HAVE YOU HEARD THE GOOD NEWS?

Visit our web site at
www.albahouse.org
(for orders www.stpauls.us)
or call 1-800-343-2522 (ALBA)
and request current catalog

Have You Heard the Good News?

REFLECTIONS ON THE SUNDAY GOSPELS

Cycle B

EDWARD T. DOWLING, SJ

ST PAULS

Library of Congress Cataloging-in-Publication Data

Dowling, Edward T., S.J.
  Have you heard the good news? : reflections on the Sunday Gospels,
cycle B / Edward T. Dowling.
    p. cm.
  ISBN 0-8189-0926-9 (alk. paper)
    1. Church year sermons. 2. Bible. N.T. Mark—Sermons. 3. Bible. N.T.
Gospels—Sermons. 4. Catholic Church—Sermons. 5. Sermons, Ameri-
can— 21st century. I. Title.

  BX1756.D69 H38 2001
  252'.6—dc21
                                                          2001018210

ISBN: 0-8189-0899-8 Have You Heard the Good News? Cycle A
ISBN: 0-8189-0926-9 Have You Heard the Good News? Cycle B
ISBN: 0-8189-0927-7 Have You Heard the Good News? Cycle C
ISBN: 0-8189-0928-5 Have You Heard the Good News? 3 Vols.

Produced and designed in the United States of America by the
Fathers and Brothers of the Society of St. Paul,
2187 Victory Boulevard, Staten Island, New York 10314-6603,
as part of their communications apostolate.

ISBN: 10: 0-8189-0926-9
ISBN: 13: 978-0-8189-0926-9

Printing Information:

Current Printing - first digit   2   3   4   5   6   7   8   9   10

Year of Current Printing - first year shown
                          2009 2010 2011 2012 2013 2014 2015

*Dedicated to
the memory of a good friend,
Donald C. Matthews, SJ*

Table of Contents

Table of Contents

Preface

This collection of homilies represents the fruit of thirty years of preaching each Sunday in parishes in the Bronx, Westchester, and Long Island. People from very different social, racial, and educational backgrounds have claimed to have enjoyed these sermons and to have profited from them. Their enthusiastic response and desire to know more about the Good News provided the motivating force behind this publication. It is my hope that these homilies will help people to understand Scripture better, appreciate it more, and read it more frequently. This book is intended for everyone who would like to be better acquainted with the Sunday readings, not merely the homilist in search of ideas for his next sermon.

I feel I should start with a disclaimer. Let me explain why. In my first twenty-nine years of preaching I never wrote out a homily. I spoke simply from notes and outlines scribbled on 3" x 5" pieces of paper. There was neither thought nor room nor perceived need for proper referencing and citations. I was speaking extemporaneously and simply trying to share with the congregation what I had learned on the topic. Over all those years whenever someone asked for a copy of a homily, I had nothing to give them for I had only jottings that were unintelligible to anyone but me. It wasn't until Advent 1998 that I first began to write out my homilies. I did so in response to lay people and nuns who said they would be helped if they had a copy of the homily to reflect on. I never thought of the possibility of publication even then until the same people urged me to try.

I am one of the least creative of God's creatures; a modest man, with much to be modest about. If I have any gift, it's as a teacher helping others to understand and come to love what I have learned and love myself. This collection of homilies owes much to many people and sources over thirty years of struggling to prepare a half-way decent homily each week. Many of the sources I regretfully cannot now adequately remember or specifically acknowledge. Let me mention, however, a few of the more unforgettable helps and influences to which I am particularly indebted.

My first inspiration came from Edward Mally, SJ, my New Testament Scripture Professor in Theology. He opened up the Sacred Text for me and taught me an approach that I have tried to emulate to this day. For the next fifteen years of preaching I muddled through pretty much on my own. Then in 1984 while helping out as a civilian chaplain to the U.S. Army in Germany, I came upon a copy of *Share the Word* whose editor at the time, Laurence F.X. Brett, was absolutely brilliant in explaining the Sunday readings, both Old and New Testaments. Each of his monthly installments helped me tremendously but I am unable now to document that help because my copies of the magazine have long since been discarded. The magazine is still a gem, however, and warrants attention.[1]

In 1995 a parish priest friend introduced me to *Homily Helps* from St. Anthony Messenger Press.[2] They have a series of reflections for both Sundays and weekdays, each of which includes sections on scriptural exegesis as well. I find the exegetical sections for weekdays particularly helpful and informative. At about the same time another priest friend told me of Mark Link's two volumes, *Illustrated Sunday Homilies*, both of which are excellent.[3] He is a master story teller whom I have used over and over but whose stories I have tried to eliminate where possible from

---

[1] *Share the Word*, Paulist National Catholic Evangelization Association, 3031 Fourth Street NE, Washington, DC 20017-1102.

[2] *Homily Helps* and *Weekday Homily Helps*, St. Anthony Messenger Press, 1615 Republic Street, Cincinnati, OH 45210.

[3] Mark Link, SJ, *Illustrated Sunday Homilies*, Tabor Publishing, 200 E. Bethany Dr., Allen, TX 75002.

the current collection. Nevertheless, people always love a good story and I can say from experience that his stories can be used effectively as introductions, conclusions, or illustrations to many of these homilies. A treasure trove for explanations and background material on both the Old and New Testaments is William Barclay's *The Daily Study Bible Series.*[4] It is suitable for both the homilist and lay person. Though all seventeen volumes are good, the six volumes on the Gospels are perhaps the most practical.

In the past few years two Jesuit friends have also shared their homilies with me. I have enjoyed and profited from their work and would like to acknowledge and thank them both: Gus Grady, SJ, has a private publication, *Searching the Sunday Scriptures,* and Bill O'Malley, SJ, a prolific author, offers a homily each week that is aimed at college students.

---

[4] William Barclay, *The Daily Study Bible Series,* Westminster Press, 100 Witherspoon St., Louisville, KY 40202.

Biblical Abbreviations

OLD TESTAMENT

Genesis	Gn	Nehemiah	Ne	Baruch	Ba
Exodus	Ex	Tobit	Tb	Ezekiel	Ezk
Leviticus	Lv	Judith	Jdt	Daniel	Dn
Numbers	Nb	Esther	Est	Hosea	Ho
Deuteronomy	Dt	1 Maccabees	1 M	Joel	Jl
Joshua	Jos	2 Maccabees	2 M	Amos	Am
Judges	Jg	Job	Jb	Obadiah	Ob
Ruth	Rt	Psalms	Ps	Jonah	Jon
1 Samuel	1 S	Proverbs	Pr	Micah	Mi
2 Samuel	2 S	Ecclesiastes	Ec	Nahum	Na
1 Kings	1 K	Song of Songs	Sg	Habakkuk	Hab
2 Kings	2 K	Wisdom	Ws	Zephaniah	Zp
1 Chronicles	1 Ch	Sirach	Si	Haggai	Hg
2 Chronicles	2 Ch	Isaiah	Is	Malachi	Ml
Ezra	Ezr	Jeremiah	Jr	Zechariah	Zc
		Lamentations	Lm		

NEW TESTAMENT

Matthew	Mt	Ephesians	Eph	Hebrews	Heb
Mark	Mk	Philippians	Ph	James	Jm
Luke	Lk	Colossians	Col	1 Peter	1 P
John	Jn	1 Thessalonians	1 Th	2 Peter	2 P
Acts	Ac	2 Thessalonians	2 Th	1 John	1 Jn
Romans	Rm	1 Timothy	1 Tm	2 John	2 Jn
1 Corinthians	1 Cor	2 Timothy	2 Tm	3 John	3 Jn
2 Corinthians	2 Cor	Titus	Tt	Jude	Jude
Galatians	Gal	Philemon	Phm	Revelation	Rv

HAVE YOU HEARD THE GOOD NEWS?

Be Alert

Today is the first Sunday of Advent, the beginning of a new liturgical year. Advent means coming or arrival. In Advent the Church asks us to prepare for the coming of the Lord. Usually we think of the coming of Jesus in terms of his birth at Christmas. But there are really three ways in which we can think of the coming of Jesus: past, present, and future. Jesus came into the world 2000 years ago when he was born in Bethlehem; he still comes into the world today, through prayer and the sacraments, to those who are willing to receive him; and he will come again on the last day to judge the world. The Church chooses today's Gospel to remind us that we will not be able to celebrate the anniversary of his coming to us at Bethlehem properly or receive him into our hearts through prayer and the sacraments worthily unless we are prepared to meet him at the final judgment. To celebrate the joy of Jesus' birth properly, we must live each and every day prepared to meet the Lord whenever he comes.

Today's Gospel is brief and seemingly simple, similar in theme to the Gospels of the last two weeks. But it is actually quite important in Mark's Gospel. We know this from four characteristics, any one of which by itself would call attention to the passage. First, it appears in Chapter 13 of Mark, the last chapter devoted to the public life of Jesus. Chapter 14 begins the Passion and Death, so this passage is one of the final teachings of Jesus before his death. As such, it warrants extra attention. Second, in setting the scene earlier in Chapter 13, Mark tells us that Jesus left the Temple area and went up the Mount of Olives with his disciples. A mountain in Scripture is frequently a place for revelation. God revealed himself to Moses on Mt. Sinai and on Mt. Sinai gave him the Ten Commandments. When Jesus began his teaching he also ascended a mountain to deliver the Sermon on the Mount, containing the core of his teaching. Thus the mountain location is a further indication that an important revelation is about to take place. Third, Mark also tells us that Jesus sat down. A seated position does not seem important today but it was in ancient times. It indicated authority. Kings sat while their subjects stood or knelt before them. Moses and the rabbis also sat when teaching formally. A remnant of this still exists in the Church. When the Pope declares a dogma of the faith, he does so *ex cathedra,* meaning from the chair of Peter. So the fact that Mark tells us Jesus sat down also indicates that the teaching to follow is important. Fourth, Mark lists the audience by name. Usually the evangelists tell us Jesus preached to the crowds or multitudes. Here he specifies the audience: Peter, James, John, and Andrew, the first four Apostles that Jesus called and the most highly regarded of the twelve. It is another way of Mark's telling us that what follows is important.

What is the point of today's Gospel? In the parable a man about to travel abroad assigns to each of his servants individual responsibilities and asks them to perform them faithfully in his absence. The man represents Jesus who will soon return to his Father after his passion and death. His servants are his disciples. The meaning of the parable suggests that Jesus has assigned to each of his disciples a task in life and asks us to fulfill that task. His farewell advice is that we be faithful to our duties in life and not grow negligent.

The theme from the reading of Isaiah is also similar. Third Isaiah wrote after the Fall of Jerusalem and the Babylonian Captivity (587-537 BC) at a time when the Jewish people were overwhelmed by the loss of their capital and Temple. They asked God how it could have happened. Isaiah finds the root of their suffering in their sinfulness and failure to live up to their covenant promises. He sees God as their only hope and so calls upon God in the people's name to come to their aid using two beautiful images: father and redeemer.

In ancient times a father was the patriarch of the extended

family, responsible for providing them with food, shelter, and protection. In Jewish society, he was responsible for maintaining the covenant with Yahweh as well. Realizing that the Jewish people have sinned and human patriarchs are inadequate, Isaiah calls upon God to be father or patriarch to the nation, both to provide for the people and to help them remain faithful to his covenant. A redeemer, on the other hand, was a member of one's family who assumed the responsibility of freeing his kinsman from slavery or debt. At a time when debt could lead to imprisonment or being reduced to the condition of an indentured servant or slave, a redeemer was anyone who saved a relative from such a fate. With the Jewish people enslaved both by foreign conquerors and their own sinful ways, Isaiah sees God as the only one powerful enough to save them and so calls upon God to act directly as their redeemer.

A subtle theological difference between the Old Testament and the Gospel is apparent here. Isaiah calls upon God to intervene externally and perform some mighty work to drive off the foreign oppressors and save his people. But the thrust of the New Testament message is for internal intervention. God has already intervened externally by sending his Son. As Christians, we simply ask now that God help us to follow in the steps of Jesus, to live up to his teachings and follow his ways.

Today's readings are also applicable to us today. We have all been given a task or mission in life that we call a vocation, be it marriage or religious life, priesthood or parenthood. God has assigned people to our care, be it family, neighbors, or needy citizens of the world. During Advent the Church asks us to pay a little extra attention to our obligations in preparation for Christmas, so that when Jesus comes he will truly find us watching in prayer and showing love for one another, just as he did in his lifetime.

John the Baptist

Today's Gospel comes from the very beginning of Mark. Though appearing second among the Gospels in the New Testament, Mark was actually written first. Mark's Gospel is the shortest, the bluntest, and the most primitive of all the Gospels. It reads like an eyewitness account, and this presents a problem. Mark was too young to have been a disciple of Jesus and to have witnessed firsthand much of what he related. So Scripture scholars surmise his Gospel is based on the recollections of St. Peter with whom Mark worked closely after the death of Jesus. Some think of Mark's Gospel as the Gospel of St. Peter, but more accurately it is the Gospel of Mark based on the recollections of St. Peter.

Mark calls his work a Gospel. This was originally a secular term meaning "good news" and was generally reserved for such special announcements as the birth of a king, a decisive victory in battle, or the inauguration of an emperor. Such reports were welcomed with great joy for they signified the beginning of a new era with new hope. Mark thus signals from the very beginning of his Gospel that Jesus will issue in a new era with new hope. Mark also gives us the reason for this hope. In his very first sentence he shares an important secret with his readers, namely that Jesus Christ is truly the Son of God. This secret, known as the Messianic secret, is left to all the other personalities in the Gospel to work out for themselves and unfortunately it eludes most of them until the very end of the Gospel. Only then, at the death of Jesus, does the Roman soldier at the foot of the cross cry out, "Indeed this was the Son of God." The good news or Gospel, then, is that the Son of God became man and laid down his life to save us.

Mark begins with a quotation from Isaiah, which cannot be identified exactly as cited. While unsettling by modern norms, it was generally accepted as commonplace in ancient times. Remember

Mark and his peers did not have easy access to sources. Scripture was nowhere gathered into one volume. Each book was handwritten on individual scrolls and the scrolls were relatively rare. Also chapter and verse notations, as we know them, were not incorporated into Scripture until the Middle Ages, further complicating identification of a text at the time. So Mark was most probably relying on memory and using a custom of the day, which involved a compilation of several texts.

The Jewish people believed that God guided them through revelation and in the person of the prophets. Yet at the time of John the Baptist, there had not been a prophet in Israel for nearly 500 years. With no prophets to guide them, devout Jews frequently looked to Scripture, God's past revelation, to guide them in the present. They regularly interpreted the present in light of the past. Using this technique to identify the role of John in God's plan for salvation, Mark in all likelihood scoured his memory of the Old Testament and came up with three prophecies particularly pertinent to John. The first is from Exodus (23:20) where God promises to send an angel (messenger of God) to lead his people in their deliverance from exile in Egypt to the Promised Land. The second is from Isaiah (40:3) which speaks of a messenger coming to announce a new exodus from the current exile of Babylon back to the Holy Land. The third comes from Malachi (3:1) where God speaks of sending a messenger to call his people back from the exile of sin to proper worship in his Temple.

Mark tells us John the Baptist began his work at the Jordan River. The Jordan is the main river in Palestine, running 135 miles from north to south but with its many meanderings stretching out over a distance of 250 miles. Its width ranges from 80 to 180 feet; its depth, from 5 to 12 feet. Just before it reaches the Dead Sea, not far from the city of Jericho, there is a relatively shallow spot in the river. From ancient times caravans and travelers from all over the Middle East have used it as a crossing point and meeting place. It may have been here that Joshua led the Jewish people into the Promised Land (Jos 3:16). At any rate, John began his public ministry somewhere in the environs.

John's message called for a baptism of repentance. This surprised the Jews because they felt they had no need of baptism. Anyone born of Jewish parents was born into the people of God by the terms of the covenant and hence was considered a child of God. Baptism was required only of converts, people who earlier in life had not known Yahweh or observed the Mosaic Law and consequently were looked upon as steeped in sin. Such people needed total immersion in baptism to be purified. In asking natural born Jews to be baptized, John reminds them and us that even children of God are fallible and in need of cleansing and being forgiven.

John's baptism was merely symbolic, however. It was an outward sign, cleansing the person from head to toe by total immersion to symbolize the inner longing of the recipient to be washed clean of sin. The rite was simply that, however: an outward manifestation and proclamation of the person's desire to repent and be forgiven. It had no intrinsic power of its own to forgive sin or restore grace. That's why John says that Jesus is greater than he. John baptized with water, which only symbolizes and invites forgiveness of sin, but Jesus baptizes with the Holy Spirit, who alone has the power to forgive sin and bestow a new life of sanctifying grace. The baptism Jesus confers is efficacious, therefore, because it alone is capable of reuniting the person once again with God.

John also called for repentance. Repentance to the Jewish mind has an almost geographical dimension. It implies the person realizes he has taken a wrong turn and deliberately reverses course 180° to redirect himself back to God. Consequently, true repentance means much more than simply regretting the past. It requires taking steps to rectify it. Anyone who is hung-over or serving time in prison has reason to regret the past and wish things were otherwise. But that is not repentance. True repentance means taking concrete action to ensure the past does not repeat itself. While this is often difficult, especially with ingrained habits or habitual sin, John offers new hope in the one who will come after him. He announces that Jesus will baptize with the Holy Spirit, which means change is possible.

So as we reflect on this Gospel, let us thank God for the good news he has given us. He has sent his only Son to live among us and open the way to the Father. Let us take John's words to heart and repent so that our lives can be totally redirected to God.

Isaiah

Today's first reading, as many of the first readings in Advent, is from the prophet Isaiah. People are sometimes surprised to learn that there was more than one Isaiah. Scripture scholars tell us there were at least three Isaiahs. And this, oddly enough, is cause for edification, not disedification.

How do we know there were three Isaiahs? Scripture scholars conclude there have to have been at least three Isaiahs from the chronology of events reported in the Book of Isaiah. The first part of the book (chs. 1-39) deals with events during the monarchy (742-687 BC); the second section (chs. 40-55) treats the exile in Babylon (587-538 BC); and the last part (chs. 56-66) speaks of the exiles' return to Jerusalem (538-500 BC). No one person could have lived long enough to cover events spanning some 250 years.

Why then only one name? Humility. Prophets felt they were merely messengers of God and who they were was not important. Only God's word, which they were commissioned to deliver, mattered. Malachi, for instance, never even told us his name. Malachi means simply, "my (God's) messenger." We also know from Old Testament times that prophets usually gathered groups of followers around them to help spread their message and keep it alive. The New Testament also reports that John the Baptist had a band of disciples and Jesus had the Apostles. Scripture scholars conclude, then, that Second and Third Isaiah were in all likelihood disciples of the previous Isaiah and merely continued his work without calling attention to themselves. The important thing was communicating God's word.

First Isaiah's task was to warn the people not to commit themselves to foreign alliances. Many at the time felt the only way to advance was to align themselves with a mightier power. Isaiah warned if they formed an alliance with pagans, they would lose their monotheism. To discourage such pacts, he wrote in chs. 6-12, called the Book of Emmanuel, messianic prophecies to proclaim God would send a king to save them. The Jewish people at the time were divided into two kingdoms. Israel, the northern kingdom consisting of ten tribes, ignored Isaiah's teaching and formed an alliance with Syria against Assyria. Assyria then moved in, conquered the ten northern tribes in 722 BC, and sent them into exile. The Assyrian form of exile was brutal. They separated all the vanquished, dispersing them throughout their far-flung empire, where isolated from each other, they would be unable to unite or rebel. Cut off from each other, their Temple and their traditions, they began to intermix, intermingle, and intermarry with their pagan neighbors and ended up eventually losing all traces of their faith and Jewish identity. As a result, they have gone down in history as the ten lost tribes of Israel.

The two southern tribes around Jerusalem, called Judah, formed an alliance with the then reigning superpower, Assyria, that saved them from immediate destruction. But it left them little more than a vassal state of Assyria for the next 150 years. Eventually they too were conquered. Babylon, the new world power, overran Jerusalem in 587 BC and sent them off into exile. Babylonian exile was not as harsh as Assyrian exile. The Babylonians exiled only the best and brightest, the ones most likely to lead a rebellion. They also selected only one or two from a family, holding them as hostages to keep those left behind in line. As long as those back home caused no problems, the exiles were free to pursue their own interests and even their own religion in Babylon. It was to these exiles that God sent Second Isaiah. His contribution (chs. 40-55), called the Book of Consolation, contains the lyrical poems known as the Servant Songs, telling of one who would lay down his life to save his people.

With the encouragement of Second Isaiah, the exiles from the southern kingdom fared better than their hapless predecessors. They learned from the sad experience of their northern neighbors and organized schools or synagogues for the very first time in order to preserve and teach their sacred Scripture. In the absence of the Temple, the synagogue also served as a place of prayer and worship. By universal reckoning, the synagogues were chiefly responsible for the preservation of Jewish faith and identity during the terrible trauma of the Babylonian exile.

After some fifty years of exile in Babylon, Second Isaiah's prophecy came true and the Jews were allowed to return to Palestine. God miraculously raised up Cyrus the Great, founder of the Persian Empire, who conquered Babylon and freed all exiles to return home. Unlike previous conquerors, he believed his empire would grow faster and more prosperous if all its components were permitted to flourish in concert. When the people returned home and saw the Temple and Jerusalem razed to the ground, however, they were devastated. Adding insult to injury, those who had been left behind and collaborated with the Babylonians had prospered in the interim.

Third Isaiah's task was to encourage the flagging spirits of the returned exiles. Just as God has delivered them from captivity, he tells them, so God would now help them to rebuild. In today's reading, Third Isaiah speaks of Jerusalem, a symbol for the Jewish people, clothed as a bride, recalling the special marital imagery that God used to describe his special love for the Jewish people. The marital imagery is a subtle reminder that just as any woman can remember her wedding day, so should they remember God's special love for them, in bad times as well as good, and not lose heart in the face of all that surrounded them. If they trust in God, Isaiah assures them, God will help them to rebuild.

Let us take Isaiah's message to heart. Through Baptism God has joined us to himself in a union far closer than marriage. He has made us his own. If we place our trust in him in good times and in bad, as Isaiah suggests, he will deepen the bond between us and help us live as true children of God, furthering the kingdom of God on earth and preparing us for our eternal reward in heaven.

The Annunciation

Luke's Gospel is often called the Gospel of Women. He tells us more about Mary and other female figures in New Testament times than all the other evangelists put together. One way he does this is by trying to balance stories about men with stories about women, indicating that women also had an important role to play in the history of salvation and that Jesus frequently tailored his message to their particular needs and concerns. We see one of these gender-balancing presentations in the overall setting of today's Gospel and we will see another shortly when the appearance of the prophet Simeon is balanced immediately by the appearance of the prophetess Anna at the presentation of Jesus in the Temple.

Luke opens his Gospel with two annunciation scenes presented in chronological order. The first is the annunciation by the Angel Gabriel to Zechariah about the birth of John the Baptist. The second is the annunciation by the same Angel Gabriel to Mary about the birth of Jesus. Luke does this to highlight the difference between Jesus and John the Baptist, and to show the contrast between Mary and Zechariah.

Let us begin with the contrast between Mary and Zechariah. Recall the respective settings. Zechariah was a priest. When the Angel Gabriel appeared to him, he was on Temple duty in Jerusalem in the Holy of Holies, the very dwelling place of God on earth, where he had been chosen by lot to offer incense. Despite his priestly status and the fact that he was in the most sacred spot of all Judaism, in the very presence of God, Zechariah found it hard to accept the angel's message. He doubted in his heart and as a result God struck him temporarily dumb. Mary, by contrast, was at home alone in a backwater town called Nazareth from which people felt no good could come. She too is startled, but despite the fact everyone believed the Messiah would be born to a princess in

11

a palace, she quickly adjusts to God's will and places herself fully at his disposal with her response, "Be it done unto me according to thy word." As a result, God, always respectful of human freedom, is free to act and put into effect his cherished plan for salvation. While Zechariah, a mature man and a priest, doubted and held back, Mary, a young girl and simple peasant, gave herself completely to God with wondrous consequences.

Gabriel tells Mary the Holy Spirit will "overshadow" her, a word used rarely in Scripture but rich in significance. It is used in Exodus (40) to describe a cloud that hovered over the Tent of Meeting in which the Ark of the Covenant was kept. Exodus (40:34) tells us that whenever the cloud "overshadowed" the tent, the Lord's presence filled it. Luke's use of the word here suggests that when Mary uttered her Fiat in acceptance of God's plan, she became the new Ark of the Covenant, bearing God's Son within her. She was destined to give him human flesh and human form so he might come into the world as one like us, though free from sin, to save us from the penalty of sin.

Let us return now to Luke's second point: the difference between Jesus and the other great people in Scripture. Note that Luke carefully crafts his annunciation scenes to adhere to the Old Testament pattern of describing the announcement of the birth of great figures in Israel's history, such as Ishmael (Gn 16:7-15), Isaac (Gn 17:1-22), and Samson (Jgs 13:1-25), individuals who all played a key role in God's plan of salvation. By using the same pattern as the Old Testament in proclaiming the birth of John and Jesus, Luke highlights the continuity between the Old Testament and New Testament and suggests that John and Jesus will likewise be important instruments of God's will.

Besides the continuity and similarities, however, Luke is anxious to point out the difference that separates Jesus from the others, notably that Jesus in person and role is greater than all who have gone before him, even John the Baptist who was the greatest of all the Old Testament prophets. Luke does this by subtly pointing out the differences between John, the subject of the first annunciation, and Jesus, the focus of the second annunciation. Note that both husband and wife, Zechariah and Elizabeth, are mentioned in the first account, indicating John would be born in the normal human way. Only Mary appears in the second account, however, with no mention of Joseph, suggesting Jesus will be born in a special way, with God intervening directly in nature so that Jesus is truly the Son of God with God alone as his Father.

On the Fourth Sunday of Advent, the Church asks us to reflect on Mary. Sometimes Mary's role in the Annunciation looks easy, as if all she had to do was say yes. But great people have a way of making the difficult look simple. I knew a woman who had five daughters and a son, all grown now. Every time they gather for the holidays, the children who each have several children of their own, still marvel at how their mother ever handled six in an era before disposable diapers and washing machines. Yet she was always unflappable, never ruffled. Everything seemed so easy and natural. The same was true of Mary. But let us never underestimate Mary's courage, faith, and trust. Try occasionally to put yourself in her place. Imagine your returning home to find an angel in your kitchen with a message for you to deliver to the president. Would you call the White House or the bureau of mental health? Improbable as it may seem, it is no more improbable than Mary's encounter with the angel and her subsequent mission. Yet Mary rose to the occasion and because of her cooperation, she brought the Savior into the world. Let us pray that we can also be Arks of the Covenant and help bring Jesus to the world through our actions and love.

The Nativity in Scripture

Christmas is the most popular feast in the liturgical calendar for most Americans. We offered a traditional homily based on the Gospel for Midnight Mass in Cycle A. It might be of interest here, therefore, to try a new tack and see how the Christmas saga evolved in history from a scriptural perspective.

Surprisingly, Christmas is mentioned in only two of the four Gospels. Mark, who wrote his Gospel first, makes no mention at all of the birth of Jesus, nor does he record any of the events of the Infancy Narrative. Rather he begins his Gospel with the public life of Jesus, starting with the baptism of Jesus by John in the Jordan. This suggests that Mark either did not know of the details surrounding the birth of Jesus or he deliberately chose to omit them. The later seems more plausible. Mark, like most in the early Church, was convinced that the central act in the life of Jesus was his passion, death, and resurrection, not his birth, and this conviction most likely dictated his decision to begin his Gospel with events more closely connected with the cross and Calvary.

The other Gospel not to mention Christmas is John. It is the Prologue of John that is read as the Gospel for Christmas Day, the same Prologue that was read as the Last Gospel each day in the old liturgy. Since John was the last to write his Gospel, he almost certainly knew the details surrounding Christmas. Yet for his own reasons he chose not to include them. Since he could assume people already knew the facts of the life of Jesus from the other evangelists, John chose instead to write a sweeping theological overview of the impact of Jesus on the history of humankind. And so rather than start with the public life or the birth of Jesus, John pushes further back into time, to the very beginning of the world. His opening words, "In the beginning was the Word," deliberately mime the beginning of the Bible itself where in Genesis (1:1) we read: "In the beginning God created heaven and earth." John's choice of imagery suggests Jesus has come to bring about a new creation, not the physical fabrication of an alternate universe, but a new world order founded on a loving relationship between God and humankind.

John's Christmas message to us is that the Word, the eternal Son of God, has united heaven and earth by assuming human flesh and living among us. By his word and example Jesus has shown us how to love God our Father. Even in his Prologue, however, John hints of trouble and the impending cross: "He came unto his own and his own received him not." John thus warns of the cross from the very outset of his Gospel and then moves directly to the events leading up to the crucifixion, starting with Jesus' public life: the call of the Apostles and his baptism by John in the Jordan River.

The two evangelists who do mention Christmas, Matthew and Luke, offer different but not contradictory accounts. A prominent feature of Matthew's recollection is the visit of the Magi, yet Luke never mentions or refers to them. Luke makes much of the presence of shepherds in the locality of Bethlehem and their role in spreading the good news, but Matthew is completely silent about them. Either Matthew and Luke were drawing from two independent oral traditions or they shared the same sources but used them differently to suit their respective theological viewpoints and personal renderings of the Gospel story. The latter is more likely.

Matthew's Nativity narrative, for instance, is tinged with sadness and foreboding. He uses the Nativity as an introduction to the Passion. Like a novelist weaving in a theme or clue at the beginning of his story that will not become clear till the end, Matthew has the Magi refer to Jesus at the very outset of his Gospel as King of the Jews. It is one of the first titles assigned to Jesus in Matthew's Gospel to indicate Jesus' purpose for coming into the world. Interestingly enough, it comes from the mouths of foreigners. Then at the end of the Gospel, as Jesus hangs upon the cross, over his head is a sign which reads "Jesus of Nazareth, King of the

15

Jews," giving the reason he was sentenced to death. Tellingly, the sign was written by Pilate, a foreigner, against the expressed will of the Jewish religious leaders. It would seem Matthew introduced the birth of Jesus into his Gospel, at least in part, to foreshadow the death of Jesus, which was truly the central act of his life and mission. It also helps to explain the unexpected note of gloom that cuts through Matthew's whole Infancy Narrative: the hostility of Herod, the indifference of the citizens of Jerusalem, the slaughter of the Holy Innocents, the need for the Holy Family to flee into Egypt.

Luke, by way of contrast, concentrates by and large on the joyful aspects of the birth of Jesus. Except for Simeon's prophecy that a sword would pierce Mary's heart and the child was destined for the fall and rise of many in Israel, Luke's account tells of the sky being lit up, an angel of the Lord appearing to the shepherds to announce the birth of Jesus, and a multitude of heavenly hosts singing God's praises. He speaks of tidings of great joy, nothing to fear, peace on earth, and most especially the good news that a Savior has been born, a Savior who is both Messiah and Lord.

In Luke's theology, the birth of Jesus, which he recounts in the beginning of his Gospel, parallels the birth of the Church, which he depicts at the beginning of his sequel to the Gospel, the Acts of the Apostles. In Luke's Nativity scene an angel appears to the shepherds with good news which is to be shared by all the people (Lk 2:10). At the start of the Acts of the Apostles, when Jesus ascends into heaven, two angels ask why the disciples remain standing by idly looking up into heaven (Ac 1:11). As soon as the Spirit descends, however, they realize their call and go out at once to spread the good news (Ac 2:4-8).

From a scriptural point of view, then, it is clear the early Church did not consider Christmas as important as the vast majority of Christians do today. The early Church concentrated the bulk of its attention on the central trilogy of events in the life of Jesus, namely, his passion, death, and resurrection. While we too cherish the concluding days of the life of Our Lord as the most important theologically, we also treasure the moment in history when it all began. We recall with particular gratitude that Jesus, the eternal Son of God, became fully human for us in order to open heaven once again and show us the way to the Father. Unlike the pagan gods of other cultures who were only said to have "appeared as" humans, Jesus truly became human and lived his life on earth as one exactly like us in all things but sin.

Simeon and Anna

The setting for today's Gospel is the Presentation in the Temple when Mary and Joseph bring the child Jesus to the Temple to dedicate their firstborn son to the Lord, indicating that they see themselves as continuing on in the Old Law and not breaking away from long-standing tradition. There they are met by Simeon the prophet who is described as awaiting the "consolation of Israel," meaning the Messianic Age. For it was in the Messianic Age that Israel was to be freed from its enemies and enjoy the consolation of once again being God's people living in peace, security, and autonomy. We are told it had been revealed to Simeon that he would not die until he had seen the Christ, which simply means the Anointed One, a synonym for the long-awaited Messiah.

Simeon takes Jesus in his arms and speaks of the Christ child as fulfilling two of Isaiah's Servant Songs. He speaks of Jesus as a "revealing light to the Gentiles," drawing from Isaiah (49:6): "I will make of you a light to the nations, that my salvation may reach to the ends of the earth." With this line Isaiah introduces an early note of universalism into salvation history, suggesting that the Messiah will come to save all people, not simply the Jews, as most Jews expected. By recounting this image of Isaiah from Simeon, Luke starts the mission of Jesus on a universal note, indicating Jesus has come to save all. Simeon also refers to Jesus as the "glory of Israel," fulfilling Isaiah (46:13): "I will put salvation within Zion and give to Israel my glory." Jesus has come to save us from sin and in so doing will restore Israel and all God's people to glory.

Looking forward into the future, Simeon sees Jesus as "destined for the fall and rise of many in Israel," meaning that those who accept Jesus will rise to a new and higher life of closer union with God, while those who reject Jesus will simply cut themselves off from grace. Simeon also foresees Jesus will be opposed in his mission. The forces of evil are so firmly entrenched in this world that even people of good will often find it hard to break clear of sin to respond to Jesus' call for perfect love. In mentioning this opposition, Luke also introduces overtones of the Cross at the very beginning of his Gospel.

Next as was frequently his custom of balancing stories about men with stories about women, Luke introduces Anna the prophetess. This reminds us that women were prophets in biblical times as well as men and indicates that women, too, had important roles to play in the history of salvation. Scripture also reveals they served as judges or charismatic leaders raised up by God to save the people (Jg 4:4). For her part, Anna is also quick to recognize the significance of Jesus. Equally important, she is the first in Luke's Gospel to act as an apostle or missionary by talking openly about the child to all awaiting the deliverance of Jerusalem.

Mention of Simeon and Anna offers an opportunity to clarify the role of a prophet. Simeon and Anna clearly do not rank among the four major literary prophets (Isaiah, Jeremiah, Ezekiel, and Daniel) who left behind significant bodies of work that were later incorporated into Scripture, nor among the twelve minor literary prophets (Hosea, Joel, Amos, Obadiah, Jonah, Micah, Nahum, Habakkuk, Zephaniah, Haggai, Zechariah, and Malachi) who left behind equally important but shorter works. Yet though relatively unknown and unrenowned and completely unpublished, Anna and Simeon nonetheless still warrant the title of prophet.

The word "prophet" comes from the Greek word προφημι, which is a composite of two words: προ, a preposition meaning either (1) *before* or *ahead of*, or (2) *on behalf of* or *for the sake of*, and φαναί, a verb meaning to *speak*. A prophet, therefore, is someone who speaks in advance of things to come or on behalf of someone else. Unfortunately, the usual English connotation of prophet leans heavily towards the first meaning, reducing the role of a prophet to little more than soothsayer or seer. But this is an insignificant part of prophecy in Scripture. A true prophet is rather one who speaks on behalf of God, one who makes God's will known and can discern in current events or circumstances the unfolding of God's plans. In short, a prophet is God's spokesperson, missioned to bring God's word to others and to help them put it into practice. In this broader sense Nathan, Samuel, Elijah, and Elisha are numbered among the great prophets of Israel, though they never published a line.

In the broadest sense, prophets were simply people such as Simeon and Anna who spoke up for God, who tried to make him and his ways known, and who tried to help others to come closer to God. In this sense, there have been many prophets over the history of time: in Old Testament times, in New Testament times, and even in our own times. In this broad sense of prophet we can think of parents, grandparents, teachers, and educators as prophets in their own way, people who try to make God known to others and to help them follow in his way. Anyone who stands up for justice, racial equality, equal opportunity, the rights of the oppressed, the needs of the underprivileged, be it at home, in the workplace, or in social gatherings, follows in the prophets' footsteps. Any time we counter a racial slur, an immoral suggestion, or a sly character assassination, we too act as a prophet.

So today as we celebrate the Feast of the Holy Family and reflect on the Gospel reading from Luke on the Presentation in the Temple, let us thank God for the gift of prophecy throughout the history of salvation, for the many men and women who gave of themselves to promote God's cause and to help draw others closer to God. Let us thank God especially for our parents, grandparents, family members, and friends who have acted as prophets for us in helping us to know and love God better. Let us also pray for the courage to assume the role of prophet in our own time so that by our lives and example we can pass on the faith to the next generation by helping them to know God more and serve him better.

The Visitation

The Gospel assigned for today's feast is the birth of Jesus which we have developed earlier. To gain scriptural insight into Mary's vital role in salvation history let us turn to Luke's beautiful account of Mary's visitation to Elizabeth. It is unusual to find in Scripture a story such as this featuring a dialogue between women. In it we see two women filled with faith acting in mutual support to help bring to fulfillment God's will. Luke clearly intends to contrast their conduct to that of their respective spouses. While Mary's husband, Joseph, and Elizabeth's husband, Zechariah, both initially doubted God's active intervention in their lives, Mary and Elizabeth place themselves fully and unreservedly at God's disposal without a moment's hesitation. Through their gracious and generous cooperation God then changed the course of human history forever.

One commentator has likened the scene to an aria in a dramatic opera. Like any good aria, it plays a critically important role in revealing the characters and advancing the plot. Like a good aria, it is also filled with memorable highlights and themes; in this case, Old Testament highlights and themes. As Luke depicts them, the two women are filled with the spirit of prophecy as they reflect on recent events in their lives and ponder what these happenings might augur in terms of the future.

Elizabeth calls Mary "blessed among women." "Blessed" was used in the Old Testament to describe women pivotal in saving the Jewish people. One such woman was Deborah who dates back to the early settling of the Promised Land. Deborah was a prophetess, which shows that in ancient Israel prophecy was bestowed on women as well as men. God also appointed Deborah a judge. Prior to the monarchy, judges were charismatic leaders charged by God to deliver the Jewish people from their enemies. When the Canaanites were oppressing the Israelites, the people went to

Deborah. She ordered Barak, another judge, to raise 10,000 men. He raised the men but refused to go into battle without her. Deborah joined the force and it was good she did for when the enemy's army had assembled before them it was Deborah who ordered Barak to attack. For her courage she was given the title "Mother of Israel." The poem celebrating her victory, called the Song of Deborah, was absorbed into the Old Testament and is considered the oldest piece of literature in Scripture (Jg 5:2-31). In this particular poem another heroine, named Jael, who finally succeeds in killing the Canaanite general, Sisera, is specifically termed "blessed" (Jg 5:24).

"Blessed" was also used of Judith (13:18) hundreds of years later at the time of the first Assyrian invasion. Holofernes, the Assyrian general, had surrounded Jerusalem and cut off its water supply. The people quickly despaired and wanted to surrender, but Judith told them to trust God. Then trusting in God herself, she slipped out of the city walls by night and beguiled her way right into the Assyrian camp, straight up to the tent of Holofernes himself. Then when he fell asleep besotted with wine, she slipped alongside his bed and cut off his head. Next morning when his troops found his headless torso in the blood-soaked bed in his tent, they panicked and fled. Thus Judith saved her people from certain destruction (Jdt 10:1-13:26).

Though Deborah, Jael, and Judith were mighty, warlike heroines, Luke doesn't hesitate to compare Mary to them. Through her quiet intercession and complete cooperation with her Son, Mary will in fact do more for God's people than any other creature. She will help to save them, not from physical death, but from eternal damnation.

Elizabeth also says, "Blessed is the fruit of your womb." This is precisely the same blessing Moses promised the Israelites if they were obedient to the voice of God (Dt 28:1-4). Mary is God's most obedient servant and it is her willing and complete obedience to God's will that wins her God's favor. This is confirmed later in the Gospel (Lk 11:27-28) when someone in the crowd calls out to Jesus, "Blessed is the womb that carried you and the breasts at which you nursed." And Jesus replies, "Rather, blessed are those who hear the word of God and observe it." Jesus' rejoinder makes it clear that Mary's greatness comes not through her biological connection of having given birth to Jesus but through her loving and willing conformity to God's will in all things.

Elizabeth likewise refers to Mary as "the mother of my Lord." In the Old Testament "Lord" was used to connote God. When Moses asked God at the burning bush who he was, God replied, "Yahweh," meaning "I am." To the Jewish mind the name was too sacred to pronounce. In its place, they used a circumlocution, Elohim, which means "Lord." Thus, in calling Mary "mother of my Lord," Elizabeth is the first person in Luke's Gospel to declare the divinity of Jesus.

Lastly, Elizabeth also proclaims, "Who am I that the mother of my Lord should come to me?" This is a subtle reference to David and his era. Jerusalem was originally a Jebusite city which David eventually conquered and made the capital of the Jewish nation. He then decided to move the Ark of the Covenant within the safety of Jerusalem's massive walls. The Ark was the receptacle of the Ten Commandments and revered as the dwelling place of God on earth. When an attendant was struck dead for irreverence during the transit, David immediately stopped the progress and cried out, "How can the Ark of the Lord come to me?" (2 S 6:9). Later, on hearing the Ark brought blessings to its temporary resting place, he went out to bring the Ark to Jerusalem, leaping and dancing for joy before it. Luke is clearly implying that Mary is the new Ark of the Covenant, with God indeed dwelling and taking flesh within her womb through the Incarnation. To show a further similarity, Luke tells us that just as David danced before the Ark with joy (2 S 6:14), so the child in Elizabeth's womb leaped for joy before Mary, quickened and blessed by the presence of God within her.

Christmas Blues

Today's Gospel is the same as for the Mass on Christmas Day. Since we have discussed the various Christmas Gospels and themes on the feast of Christmas itself, I thought we might try something different here and address some problems and difficulties that many people have during the Christmas holidays but most are too embarrassed or ashamed to admit. Simply knowing that others share the same problem and that one is not unique or alone with the difficulty often provides much needed help and relief to those afflicted.

Though differing slightly in character and form, the problems can generally be listed under the general heading of holiday blues. Christmas is or is supposed to be the happiest time of the year. It is a time of gift-giving and family get-togethers, a time of delicious meals and plenty of good cheer, a time bursting with memories of the past and bubbling over with hope and promise for the future. Everything is festive, everyone merry and in a holiday mood. That's what we expect of others and what others expect of us. But many fall far short of the norm and the things they so desperately long for.

In our culture Christmas is a time for giving gifts. Parents are pressured to measure up to the expectations of their children and the frequently outrageous standards set by manufacturers' ingenuity and advertisers' creativity. Parents who are having a bad year or who have to struggle perennially to keep from sinking deeper into debt face a particularly difficult time. They often experience a deep sense of inadequacy and feel they have failed to provide properly for their offspring. A disappointed child on Christmas morning can break a parent's heart and lead to self-loathing and depression on the parents' part that is unwarranted and uncalled for. In traditional families the onus falls more heavily on the male, and even affluent fathers sometimes feel guilty for not doing more. We have all been conditioned and contaminated by a system that equates one's love for others with what one is willing to spend on them. We should recognize this media manipulation for what it is and not allow the base commercialism of our society to mar our holidays.

Christmas is also a time for large festive family dinners. In addition to the cleaning, shopping, and gift wrapping, the woman of the house is expected to turn out a gourmet meal with all the traditional trimmings, frequently for the whole extended family. In many Italian families, the Christmas Eve meal is a sumptuous feast involving more than a dozen fish dishes. Any woman would be hard pressed under the best of circumstances to turn out such a feast, but Christmas Eve with the decorating of the tree and the house makes it doubly difficult. Many taking on the challenge are grandmothers anxious to have the whole family together and traditions maintained the way their mothers did. But it's been a long time since they've cooked for a crowd and their organizational skills and timing in the kitchen have frequently grown rusty over time. When put under too much pressure and asking too much of ourselves, we all tend to get cross and cranky and mothers and grandmothers are no exception. They need to set realistic expectations for themselves and not become depressed because they are not the equal of superwoman. No one is measuring them against their mothers or grandmothers but themselves. The grandchildren certainly are not and their own children are appreciative of their efforts.

Christmas often brings the extended families on both sides together for the holidays. For those with in-law problems this can be particularly nerve-wracking and trying. Just when one wants to relax, one has to be on his or her best behavior. And there's so much that in-laws on both sides can manage to find fault with on the holidays: the gifts exchanged, the dinner selection, the state of the house, the brand of beer. There's also the perennial problem of whose parents to spend Christmas with when the children are younger and the equally vexing problem of prying the children away from their gifts to go anywhere else when they are older. Many a battle has been fought when peace and tranquility should reign.

Guidelines need to be established and maintained. Grandparents must share and children must learn to think of others.

Office parties and social invitations also abound during the Christmas season. At business and in the neighborhood we are called on to share food and drink. For people with a weight or drinking problem this proves to be a tense rather than a relaxing pastime. While most people are able to be at ease and enjoy the company and conviviality, people who have reason to be concerned over what they eat or drink are set immediately on edge. They try to appear nonchalant but inside they can be churning. What to others is fun, is to them a challenge, with a possible outcome they don't even want to think about. And should they slip, there's anger and self-recrimination that robs them and their families of the holiday spirit. No one should ever push food or drink on anyone. Party planners should be careful to have an assortment of low-calorie foods and non-alcoholic beverages readily available and easily accessible.

Even the weather can conspire against us at Christmas time. In many parts of the country it is cold, wet, slushy. We often can't get to the stores when we need to shop or to social or family gatherings that we long to attend. The kids can be snowed or rained in, making everyone stir-crazy; or there can be an absence of snow, leaving new sleds stranded forlornly under the tree and skiers confronted with cancelled vacations. We can't control nature and we should never allow it to control us. Weather should never influence the barometer of an individual's or family's good cheer.

There are many problems and pressures we face during the holidays. There is no way we can avoid them all. But sometimes it helps to know we are not the only ones facing these problems, we are not alone in our struggles.

Herod and the Magi

"Epiphany" means "revelation" and today we celebrate the revelation of the Christ child to the non-Jewish world in the person of the Magi. In today's Gospel Matthew deliberately contrasts Herod and the Magi. Who was Herod and who were the Magi? There are two Herods in the Gospel narrative. The Herod we read about today at the beginning of Matthew's Gospel, called the Infancy Narrative, was Herod the Great. The Herod who appears at the end of the Gospel during Our Lord's passion when Pilate sends Jesus to Herod for interrogation is Herod the Great's son, Herod Antipas (Lk 23:7-14). Herod Antipas or Herod the Younger is the one who married his brother's wife, Herodias, and had John the Baptist beheaded for condemning the union (Mt 14:1-12).

Herod the Great from today's Gospel, was a great builder. He built an aqueduct for the perennially parched city of Jerusalem and large sections of the wall and fortifications for Jerusalem and the Temple. He rebuilt Samaria, the old capital of the northern kingdom when Israel split off from Judah, and created a brand new, sprawling metropolis, named Caesarea in honor of Caesar, on the Mediterranean coast. There he constructed a huge artificial harbor to overcome the dire lack of natural harbors along the coast. He also built elaborate palaces on difficult terrain, such as jagged mountain peaks and windswept promontories jutting far out into the sea, both to capture the breathtaking views and take advantage of the unassailable protection they afforded. When ancient ruins were discovered not long ago in the Holy Land, one on a mountaintop, the other at the edge of the sea, archeologists quickly surmised they were the legacy of Herod the Great (*The New York Times,* December 15, 1992, Sec. C, p. 7).

Herod the Great was a ruthless man. He was a vassal king of the Romans and did their bidding slavishly. He was insanely jealous of his throne and killed anyone he saw as a potential threat. He killed his own wife Miriam, and when her mother had the temerity to complain of her daughter's death, he had her executed as well. As a mother-in-law, she might have known better. Herod also killed three of his six sons starting with the oldest, Antipater. Herod the Younger survived because he was away in Rome being educated in the imperial court. It was Rome's custom to bring the children of its vassal kings to Rome to study, both to educate them in the diplomacy of the Empire and to acquaint them with the Roman nobility whom they would one day serve when they ascended the throne back home. But the practice had a darker undercurrent in that the children also served as hostages, held in Rome to keep their parents in line and in Rome's orbit, doing Rome's bidding. Any trouble back home and the children would pay dearly for their parents' folly.

Caesar Augustus knew Herod's two oldest sons from their time of study in Rome. When they returned home only to be executed by their father who feared they had developed premature aspirations for his throne while in Rome, Caesar quipped sardonically it was better to be Herod's pig than to be Herod's son, playing upon the similarity of the Greek words 'υοσ for pig and 'υιοσ for son.

When an old man, knowing death was near, Herod the Great ordered the arrest of a number of the most prominent and beloved citizens of Jerusalem. Knowing no one would mourn his passing, he signed a warrant ordering their death immediately upon his own. It was his sick way of insuring that Jerusalem would have good reason to weep when he died. No crocodile tears for him. We also know from the Gospel that he ordered the death of all the male children under two years of age in the whole vicinity of Jerusalem and Bethlehem, an estimated two thousand in number, in order to eliminate any potential threat to his throne. He made Idi Amin look like a Sunday school teacher.

As for the Magi, we know little about them from history, save for tradition and legend. From history we know the Magi were a priestly caste in Persia who devoted themselves to religion and the study of science, which in those days meant the study of the stars. Stars at the time were commonly thought to announce the birth of important people. So when they saw a new star on the horizon, they set off at once in search of a newborn king. They are in a sense the first recorded instance of someone using nature to come to a deeper knowledge of God. In a Christian sense they are important as the first recorded instance of the God of Israel revealing himself to the non-Jewish world.

Interestingly enough, stars are still used for navigation in the desert. An oil executive on a visit to the Middle East once rented a jeep and drove off into the desert to explore on his own. He soon became disoriented and hopelessly lost, however, as night began to fall. Luckily he happened upon a Bedouin and asked for directions. The Bedouin smirked in disbelief and said, "Just follow that star!"

Legend tells us the names of the Magi were Melchior, Caspar, and Balthasar, with Balthasar being a person of color. Their gifts were gold, frankincense, and myrrh, all priceless in their day. Gold is a symbol for kingship. Frankincense or incense, long used in worship, is a symbol for divinity. Myrrh, a staple at funerals to mask odors, is a symbol for humanity. Jesus, a king, is both God and man. The three gifts also fulfill Psalm 72:10 which tells of the arrival of kings bearing gifts and Isaiah 60:6 which speaks of camels bearing gold and frankincense to Zion. The main point behind the story in Matthew, however, is to contrast the apathy of the Jewish world, which should have been prepared to welcome Jesus as the Messiah, with the zeal of the Magi, who though pagan, went to great lengths to discover the Christ Child and pay him homage. In short, Matthew reports sadly that his people did not know when salvation was at hand while foreigners of non-Jewish origin, the Magi, did. Today on the great feast of the Epiphany, let us pray that we not be caught napping like the people of Jerusalem but respond fully to God's love and call.

Jesus is Baptized

Today's Gospel is from Mark and it is from Mark that we will read predominantly this liturgical year. It might be good, then, to understand something of Mark's structure and style. Today's passage comes from the beginning of Mark and it is interesting to note that Mark starts his Gospel with the baptism of Jesus and not his birth. Though seemingly abrupt and not as immediately attractive as the beginning of Matthew's or Luke's Gospels with their rich details of the Infancy Narrative or as compelling as the sheer poetry that marks the start of John's Gospel, Mark nonetheless managed to capture the early Church's attention immediately and completely. To understand how, we need to recall something of the Jewish world at the time, the world from which the early Church sprang. That world was distinguished by three important characteristics.

First, the ancient Jewish world conceived of God as dwelling in the heavens and humankind inhabiting the earth, with the sky acting as a barrier or buffer between God's realm in the heavens and our human habitat on earth. At the time Jesus came, the Jewish people felt that heaven was closed to them because they had suffered a series of humiliating and debilitating defeats in battle. They had been conquered or come under the domination of first the Assyrians, next the Babylonians, then the Greeks, and finally the Romans, who currently occupied their land. They felt as if God had shut the heavens against them and abandoned them to their enemies. Against a hauntingly similar background of the sky being locked tight against them, Isaiah had earlier prayed that God would tear open the heavens and come down to save his people (63:19).

Second, it was a time that God's Spirit was absent from the world. In times past when the Jewish people were in need, God had raised up great men and women on whom he sent his Spirit, men like Moses and David, women like Deborah and Judith, who subsequently saved their people from their enemies and brought them God's peace. For many years before Jesus came there had been no great leaders, no charismatic figures, no one blessed with God's Spirit capable of delivering them.

Third, there had been no prophet in Israel for over four hundred years, no one to bring them God's word. It was as if the voice of God had been stilled in the land, his message no longer heard. God had broken off communications and the silence was deafening, reminiscent of the time Isaiah pleaded plaintively with God, asking how long God could be silent (64:11).

Against this demoralizing but popular perception that (1) the heavens were closed, (2) the Spirit was absent, and (3) the voice of God was silent, Mark begins his Gospel with the Baptism of Jesus and galvanizes his audience with the extraordinarily good news that after all these years (1) the sky is finally opened, (2) the Spirit descends, and (3) the voice of God is once again heard in the land. With these two lines Mark undoes the malaise that has been plaguing the people for years and issues in a new era of hope. Jesus is God's beloved. In sending his own Son, God has broken down the barrier between heaven and earth. The Spirit of God has descended upon Jesus, ensuring he will have the power to lead and save his people. God's voice has once again been heard and Jesus, as the perfect revelation of the Father, will continue to communicate God's word and message to the waiting world.

The proclamation from heaven, "You are my beloved Son; with you I am well pleased," expresses divine approbation of Jesus and is a blend of two scriptural texts that help to explain who Jesus is and what he will do. The first comes from Psalm 2:7, "You are my son, this day I have begotten you," which spoke originally of the Messiah whom all were expecting. The second, "With you I am well pleased," also translated as "On you my favor rests," comes from the fourth of Isaiah's Servant Songs describing a Suffering Servant who will please God by his total obedience (Is 42:1). The heavenly accolade thus suggests from the very beginning of the Gospel that

Jesus is the Messiah and that he will be a suffering Messiah.

In today's brief passage and the three lines immediately following it, Mark also implies Jesus is the new Israel and that with his Baptism he forms a new people of God. In Exodus (4:22-23), speaking collectively of the Jewish people, God had Moses tell Pharaoh, "Israel is my son, my firstborn. Hence I tell you: Let my son go, that he may serve me." Israel was subsequently freed and miraculously walked through the waters of the Red Sea on its way to becoming a new nation after undergoing forty years of trial, temptation, and unfortunately frequent failure in the desert. Here Jesus, the new Israel, emerges from the waters of baptism and sees the heavens open and God declare him his Son.

Mark next tells us Jesus is immediately led into the desert to be tried and tested for forty days where, unlike Israel, he emerges victorious. Mark then ends his brief temptation scene of Jesus using terms reminiscent of the Garden of Eden where God gave Adam and Eve dominion over all the plants and animals of creation (Gn 1:28). Here Mark tells us simply that Jesus co-existed peacefully with the wild animals in the desert and was ministered to by the angels. The point Mark is making boils down simply to this. Jesus is the new Israel, the true and ever obedient Son of God, so perfectly obedient that he introduces a new order marking the beginning of a new creation. In Jesus the kingdom of God has truly come and is open to all who are willing, through baptism, to follow Jesus and become his disciples in word and in fact.

Call of the Apostles

My Irish aunt married a Jewish man. Despite the difference in religion and backgrounds it proved a very happy marriage. My aunt was very religious and prayed night and day for her husband's conversion. She even enlisted the help of the extended family. More novenas were said, more candles lit, than one could ever imagine. But the years went by and nothing ever happened. Though all the children were raised as Catholics, her husband never expressed interest in becoming a Catholic himself.

Then one day when he was on in years and alone in the house, a nun came to the door conducting the parish census. He invited her in and she began by asking the names of all in the house, then their religions. He replied, "They're all Catholic, but me." She took her reading glasses off, looked him straight in the eye, and asked, "And you, why aren't you a Catholic?" He replied, "Because no one ever asked me." "Well I'm asking," she retorted, as only a nun in those days could. "Would you like to become a Catholic?" "Yes, very much so," he said, without doubt or hesitation. She signed him up on the spot for instructions and he was baptized soon thereafter.

My aunt was in seventh heaven. You could have knocked her over with a feather. We had all prayed so hard and so long, but not one of us had ever thought of asking. If the faith is the single most important gift God has given us, why are we so reluctant to discuss it and share it with those we love?

The theme in today's liturgy is sharing the faith. In the first reading we see the old priest Eli sharing his faith and knowledge of the Lord with the young Samuel. In the second reading we see St. Paul sharing his belief and knowledge of God's ways with the people of Corinth. In the Gospel we see Andrew sharing his new-found faith with his brother Simon. If Eli had not shared his faith with Samuel, Israel would not have had the effective transitional leader it needed between the age of the Judges and the era of the monarchy. If St. Paul had not shared his faith with the Corinthians and the non-Jewish world, whole nations and peoples, including our forebears, may never have heard of Jesus Christ. If Andrew had not shared his faith with his brother Simon, there might have been a different successor to Jesus. Sharing our faith is so important we should never hesitate to do so, particularly with family and children.

Today's Gospel is one of only three passages that tell of the apostle Andrew. Each time we meet him, he is bringing someone to Jesus. Here at the beginning of the Gospel we see him bring his brother Peter to Jesus. In the middle of the Gospel we see him bring a young boy to Jesus with five loaves and two fish which Jesus then proceeds to use for his largest and most public miracle, the Multiplication of the Loaves and Fish (Jn 6:8). Near the end of the Gospel we see him introduce to Jesus a delegation of Greeks, who were non-Jews, so Jesus can explain to them the conditions of becoming disciples (Jn 12:20-22). Thus Andrew from the very first acts as a missionary, one on fire to bring others to Jesus.

In today's Gospel two of John's disciples begin to follow Jesus. They don't have the courage to approach him directly. But they don't have to. Jesus turns to welcome them. So it is in life. If we truly seek God, no matter what our condition, God will not remain distant or aloof. He will welcome us with open arms, just as the father in the Parable of the Prodigal Son, who runs out to greet his son before his son ever has a chance to offer a formal apology. Jesus asks them, "What are you looking for?" A good question, one he asks of each and every one of us. What are we looking for? For some it's security. But if we seek security solely in material things, it is illusory. The only true security comes from loving God and doing his will. For others it's a career, to make the most of life and one's talents. But if it is all self-centered, it is hollow. Only a career that conforms to God's ways and is of service to others makes lasting sense. Still others seek peace and happiness. But as

St. Augustine reminds us, "Our hearts will never be happy and at peace until they rest in you, O Lord."

Today's Gospel comes from John who wrote for a non-Jewish audience. This explains why he frequently finds it helpful to translate Jewish words and titles. "Rabbi" means literally the "great one," but students used it so often for their teachers, that it came simply to mean "teacher." John also tells us "Messiah" means "anointed." In ancient times those specially chosen by God were anointed. Priests were anointed, as were kings. The Messiah was to be specially chosen by God and many expected him to be a priestly or kingly figure. The Greek word for "anointed," and hence also for the Messiah, is *Christos*, which we simplify in English to Christ. So Jesus Christ literally means Jesus the Anointed or Jesus the Messiah. Christ is not a surname, as some mistakenly surmise.

In today's Gospel Jesus gives Simon a new name. In the Old Testament a change of name meant a new commission by God. Abram became Abraham (father of many) when God formed a covenant with him and promised that his descendants would be as numerous as the sand on the seashore. Jacob became Israel (God rules) because he was the immediate ancestor of the twelve tribes whom God would rule as his own people. Here Jesus changes Simon's name to Peter (Rock), for it is on Peter that Jesus will one day build his Church as on a rock.

Recall the theme of vocation central to today's liturgy. Vocation involves a following and seeking, a desire to find and come to the place where the Lord dwells and to be with him. Through our Baptism we are all called to follow God more closely, be it in the priesthood or religious life, single life or married life, helping and being helped by a spouse or each other. Let us pray that we follow God faithfully and fully in whatever way of life we have chosen.

The Book of Jonah

Today's first reading comes from the Book of Jonah. Since we read from it so rarely, I thought it might be good to locate it in the Hebrew Scriptures and say a few words about its meaning.

The Hebrew Scriptures are generally divided into three main categories: the Law, the Prophets, and the Writings, which include the Wisdom Literature. The Historical Books are generally subsumed under the Prophets since they chronicle the careers of the early prophets such as Nathan, Samuel, Elijah, and Elisha. At first glance one might be tempted to classify Jonah with the Wisdom Literature for it appears to be no more than an extended narrative with an important message. But in point of fact, the Book of Jonah is listed with the Prophets even though Jonah is totally unlike any of the other prophets. The book is perhaps best understood as a prolonged parable.

A parable, as you know from the Gospels, is a story about a person or event, real or imaginary, to whom the audience can relate, that is then used to explain some facet of God or his ways. A parable also frequently involves a hidden comparison with someone in the audience that does not become obvious until the moral of the story is drawn. Casting the story in terms of an anonymous third party allows the audience to listen objectively without putting up defenses and frees them to pass judgment impartially. It is only when the moral of the story is evident that some or all in the audience realize the story is about them.

To understand the parable, we need only recap the story. Jonah is called by God to preach repentance to the Ninevites. Most prophets accepted God's call reluctantly; some, like Isaiah, from a feeling of unworthiness; others, like Jeremiah, from fear of what might happen. Jonah, however, has the unique but dubious distinction of refusing God outright, and for the basest of reasons. Nineveh was the capital of Assyria, the superpower that had destroyed the northern kingdom of Israel in 722 BC and doomed its ten tribes to a devastating exile from which they never recovered or returned. Like most Jews, Jonah so detested the Ninevites that he appears constitutionally unable and unwilling to help Israel's arch enemy even though God himself has directed otherwise. In an act of blatant defiance, Jonah goes to the port city and instead of booking passage for Nineveh in the east, deliberately signs on to a ship bound for Tarshish in Spain to the west, considered the extreme opposite end of the world to the Hebrew mind.

At sea a terrible storm threatens the ship and the sailors suspect God is punishing someone on board. They draw lots to see who it is and Jonah is singled out. Jonah then confesses he is disobeying and fleeing from his God, so the sailors toss him into the sea as an act of propitiation. Jonah is swallowed by a whale, and three days later the whale spews him up on the very shores of Nineveh. This adds a comic tone, suggesting even the whale can't stomach Jonah. It also introduces a note of ridicule. Though a dumb beast, the whale at least knows how to follow God's directions and, unlike Jonah, find its way to Nineveh.

It is here that today's reading begins with God for the second time commanding Jonah to preach repentance to the Ninevites. With heavy heart and leaden feet, Jonah embarks upon his mission, hoping against hope no one will hear him or heed him. But to his deep disgust and utter dismay, everyone from the king on down repents at once, leading God to relent and stay his punishment. The book ends with Jonah complaining bitterly to God and asking for death, still opposed to God's wish to save all people, including Israel's enemies.

What does the parable mean? On one level, the parable compares Israel to the Ninevites, offering Israel a mirror to examine itself. If the Ninevites, a pagan people with no history of revelation or God's active salvific intervention, could respond so fully and enthusiastically to a single prophet as terrible as Jonah, what should Israel have done in response to the series of great prophets God had directed its way? Yet in point of fact the Jewish people had largely ignored, often abused, and at times even killed God's personal envoys. In short, the Book of Jonah is a call to Israel to examine its conscience and behavior in light of God's repeated attempts to call them back to their original covenant love.

On another level, the parable can also be viewed as a comparison between Israel and Jonah. The Book of Jonah is one of the strongest declarations in the Old Testament of the universality of God's saving love. As Isaiah proclaimed and post-exilic theology explained, God intended the exile, in part, to make the Jewish people a light to the nations (Is 42:6) and an instrument to lead all people to himself (Is 51:4-5). But, like Jonah, the Jewish people balked at God's plan and did not want to share God's love with the Gentile world. Like Jonah, here a figure of ridicule, they tried to thwart God's plan and refused to act as a beacon guiding and attracting others to God by following the commandments and living up to their covenant promises. In this interpretation of the parable, the Book of Jonah challenges them to examine their exclusiveness and lack of universal concern for others.

Two closing thoughts. The Book of Jonah was also meant to shock its audience with its praise of the wholehearted repentance and subsequent forgiveness of Nineveh, a city which the Jews detested, much as Jesus later shocked the people in his audience when he singled out a Samaritan, a hated enemy of the Jews, as the one who truly showed love of God and love of neighbor (Lk 10:29-37). Second, the Book of Jonah also figures prominently in the New Testament as a prefigurement for the death and resurrection of Jesus. When the scribes and Pharisees ask Jesus for a sign that he is truly who he says he is, Jesus replies, "An evil and unfaithful generation seeks a sign, but no sign will be given it except the sign of Jonah" (Mt 12:39). By this Jesus means that just as Jonah was buried in the belly of the whale for three days, so he (Jesus) will be buried in the bowels of the earth for three days before rising from the dead. This will be the irrefutable sign that he is the God of all creation, the God of the living and dead.

Jesus Teaching in the Synagogue and Driving Out an Unclean Spirit

Today's Gospel is from Mark. A key question running all through Mark's Gospel is, "Who is this Jesus of Nazareth?" Mark answers the question for his readers in the very first line of his Gospel when he tells us Jesus is the Son of God, but everyone else in the Gospel narrative is left to discover it on his or her own. Today's passage offers valuable and helpful clues to the correct answer to this all-important question.

Authors have always used literary devices to structure their stories and narratives. Fairy tales typically begin with "Once upon a time" and end with "happily ever after." Jokes regularly start with "Did you hear the one about" and end with the punch line. Modern writers usually begin with the key idea and work down from it or save the best point for last and build up to it. Ancient authors, however, used many methods, one of which was placing the key element in the middle of the passage to create what commentators generally call a necklace effect.

If you hold a fine necklace of precious stones at both ends, you will typically find the most important gem in the middle, flanked by a perfectly matched pair of slightly smaller stones. Each subsequent gem is progressively smaller and perfectly paired to its corresponding counterpart on the other side, resulting in one side of the necklace being a mirror image of the other. In biblical writing, authors used similar techniques. They frequently set their central idea in the middle of the passage, leading up to it with a crescendo of details rising in importance and then moving away from it with a series of counterbalancing points presented in descending order. Today's Gospel offers a fine example of this necklace technique.

The central message in today's passage from Mark is that Jesus is "the Holy One of God." It is flanked, like the key gem in a necklace, by four couplets each carefully paired. (1) Immediately before it, the unclean spirit *cries* out, "Have you come to destroy us?" Immediately after it, the unclean spirit leaves the man with a loud *cry*. The first matched couplet is thus paired by the word *cry*. (2) Before the unclean spirit spoke, we were told, "The people were *astonished* at his (Jesus') teaching." After the unclean spirit leaves, we are told, "All who looked on were *amazed*." The second couplet is matched by feelings of *awe*. (3) Towards the beginning of the account when Jesus was teaching in the synagogue, we read Jesus "*taught* them as one having *authority* and not as the scribes." Towards the end of the story, after the miracle, people ask, "What is this? A new *teaching with authority*." The third couplet is united by the idea of "*teaching with authority*." (4) The story begins with Jesus entering the synagogue to teach or *disseminate* his message. It ends with the report that "his fame *spread* everywhere throughout the whole region of Galilee." The final couplet centers on *spreading* the good news. Knowing Mark's method helps us to appreciate his careful craftsmanship and leads us straight to the central point in the passage: Jesus is the Holy One of God.

Synagogues did not come into existence until the destruction of the Temple in 587 BC. As long as the Temple stood, it remained the sole place of public worship. The ten northern tribes were conquered and exiled by the Assyrians in 722 BC. Cut off from Temple worship, they eventually lost their faith and are known as the ten lost tribes of Israel. When the two remaining southern tribes suffered a similar fate at the hands of the Babylonians in 587 BC, they learned from the sad experience of their northern neighbors and established synagogues for the first time. Synagogues were originally schools to preserve and teach Scripture and to gather the people for prayer. Their success in preserving the faith of the Jews in exile led to their spread through Palestine on their return home. Synagogues were particularly helpful in areas far removed from the Temple in Jerusalem.

Synagogue services consisted of prayers, Scripture readings, and explanations of these readings. At the time of Jesus there were no resident rabbis. Anyone versed in the Old Testament could be asked to interpret the Scripture passage. Scribes, whose job it was to transcribe and explain Scripture, were often selected. They taught by simply passing down what they had learned in school from the great rabbis. The more they quoted, the more authoritative their teaching was thought to be. When Jesus taught, however, he broke new ground and gave fresh interpretations. Unlike the scribes, he taught on his own authority and made new law, indicating he was greater than Moses and the equal of God, who alone can bind under conscience.

Having taught with authority, like God himself, Jesus then shows by his actions he is the equal of God. In biblical times sickness was regarded as possession by the devil. Only God could cure sickness because only God had power over the devil. In curing the sick man Jesus clearly shows he has power reserved to God alone. But Mark, more than any other evangelist, frequently goes out of his way to stress demoniac possession. In doing so he emphasizes the cosmic struggle between Jesus and Satan. For Mark, Jesus is not merely curing an individual with each miracle he performs, he is decisively beating back the forces of evil and introducing the kingdom of God.

The unclean spirit addresses Jesus as the Holy One of God. In ancient times knowing a person's name was thought to provide power over the person. The unclean spirit tries to use that power to gain an advantage over Jesus but Jesus proves too powerful for the ploy and decisively drives him away, proving once again his power is greater than any other, even the powers of hell. It is also interesting that here, and all through Mark's Gospel, the demons always know immediately who Jesus is and fear him accordingly, while the ordinary people, including the Apostles, continue to wonder who Jesus is and what type of man he might be.

The Book of Job

The Book of Job was written sometime after the unspeakable suffering of the Babylonian conquest and exile (587-537 BC) in which Jerusalem was razed, the Temple destroyed, and the people packed off to pagan Babylon like pawns. The Book of Job examines the time-honored traditional religious teachings about suffering found in both Scripture and rabbinical teaching and finds them all wanting.

Job is the story of a rich and upright man whom God allows to be tested by Satan to see if he will remain faithful even under severe duress. In a series of disasters, his flocks, his wealth, even his children are all destroyed. He himself is then brought low by a repulsive, painful disease. He naturally wonders why all this has happened to him and cries out to God. His wife prods him from the start to curse God, but he will not. Four friends then come to counsel him, offering various refinements of the basic tenet of the then prevailing theology that runs all through the Deuteronomic literature, namely, that God always rewards the just and punishes the evil.

In a series of lengthy and repetitive discourses alternating between Job and each of his friends in turn, Job's suffering is discussed. Eliphaz begins his argument from reason. Since God is all just, he must reward the good and punish the evil. If Job has suffered, therefore, he must have sinned. God, also referred to as Shaddai in the book, must be punishing Job for something he did. Eliphaz tells Job to repent and God will forgive him. But Job answers honestly he has done nothing wrong. His conscience is clear. Bildad then continues and refines the argument in response to Job's denial of wrongdoing by drawing on the majesty of God. God is so far above humankind that perhaps Job does not realize his offense. Job must have done something wrong, even if inadvertently, to be punished as he is. For God only punishes evildoers. Job re-examines his conscience. Still finding nothing, he reaffirms his innocence.

Zophar next takes up the argument and continues in much the

same vein. The best he can conclude is that if Job has done nothing wrong, God may be punishing him to keep him from some future sin such as pride or arrogance. Yet this is not in Job's nature. His manifold blessings have never detracted from his love or service of God. Lastly, in what seems to be a later addition to the book, a young man named Elihu speaks up. Firmly rooted in the traditional theology, Elihu is disgusted with his older colleagues for failing to vindicate God effectively and decisively against Job. He argues once again from God's majesty and justice, and if he offers Job any concession, it is simply that God intends trials to build up character. Thus, while all four friends argue as passionately and persuasively as theological thinking to that point allowed, they fail to convince Job or adequately address his situation.

Finally God appears and vindicates Job against his friends. Job has done nothing to deserve the misery that has engulfed him. Traditional theology, as argued mightily by Job's friends, cannot explain the enigma of suffering. Worse, it created a false sense of values that fostered a perverse perception of the real order. In adhering rigidly to the notion that God must reward the good and punish the evil within the limited time frame of this world's horizons, traditional theology ended up inverting the real order and depicting God at the service of humankind, not humankind at the service of God. For in terms of this theology, humankind ultimately determines God's course of action by its behavior. Being good forces God to compensate us with rewards; being bad compels God to punish us for our sins. Though nobly intended to preserve God's majesty, the prevailing theology ended up perversely sapping God's autonomy.

God also reveals, however, that Job is not in the right against God. Job can't hold up his good works and demand a reward from God or rely on his upright behavior as a guarantee against all misfortune in life. To remind Job of his place, God simply asks, "Where were you when I founded the earth?" (38:4). "Do you know the ordinances of the heavens?" (38:33). "Would you condemn me that you may be justified?" (40:8). Job humbly admits his ignorance and, repudiating his former hubris, acknowledges he is the creature, God the creator. He accepts the mystery of God and his ways in his life with as firm a faith as he accepted his suffering.

His friends are chastised by God meanwhile for trying to fit God's manner of behavior to a simplistic formula and not leaving room for uncertainty and mystery. They were so eager to defend God's ways, which they mistakenly thought had to follow human logic, that they misjudged their friend and made his suffering worse by refusing to accept his innocence and accusing him of sins he had not committed. In their desire to defend God, who needs no defender, they created a system of theological cause and effect which was totally inadequate to the problem of suffering. As human experience attests, the good do not necessarily prosper in this life nor do the evil always suffer. To imply otherwise is to impose an unjust and intolerable burden on those already saddled with heavy crosses in life.

The flaw in the traditional theology of that day was its finite time frame. The Jewish people had no notion of eternal life at this point in history. Ironically, the problem of suffering would eventually lead them to belief in an afterlife in which God's justice would be totally vindicated (cf. Fourth Sunday of Easter, Cycle C). All the author of Job could do at the time, however, was to assure innocent people that suffering was not inexorably connected to sin or necessarily a sign of God's displeasure. Though an important conceptual breakthrough that offered some relief to those heavily burdened in life, the idea unfortunately took centuries to gain popular acceptance. Even the Apostles in the time of Jesus were not completely convinced of it. John (9:2) reports them asking Jesus, "Rabbi, who sinned, this man or his parents, that he was born blind?" The Pharisees, as one might expect, held an even stronger view, accusing the poor man of being "born totally in sin" (Jn 9:34).

Curing a Leper

Unlike Matthew who begins the Public Life of Jesus with an extended exposition of his teaching as set forth in the Sermon on the Mount, Mark begins his account of Jesus' ministry with a series of miracles. He mentions in passing that Jesus went about teaching and preaching, but he deliberately delays specifying what Jesus taught save for the cryptic catchall, "The kingdom of God is at hand. Repent and believe the good news" (Mk 1:15). Nevertheless, from the very first miracle, Mark basically depicts each cure as a "teaching with authority." Miracles demonstrated the power of God at work in Jesus. With sickness regarded as possession by the devil, Mark portrays Jesus beating back the forces of evil and establishing the reign of God with every miraculous cure.

Today's cure involves leprosy. Leprosy was the most dreaded of all diseases in ancient times. It was inherently fatal, terribly disfiguring, and totally debilitating. It robbed people of life, limb, and liberty. It ruined people's lives irreparably and consigned them to a living death in all the important areas of life. Physically, there was no known cure for leprosy. So all the leper had to look forward to was pain, disfigurement, and death. Spiritually, with sickness viewed as a punishment for sin, lepers were made to feel like sinners. Psychologically, they could expect no sympathy or compassion. Since illness was considered a direct result of sin, people judged them somehow responsible for their own afflictions. Worse, each had to face the incredible guilt trip and lingering doubt of having caused his own suffering. Socially, with leprosy considered contagious and no cure available, people shunned lepers and forced them to live as outcasts on the outskirts of civilization.

Given what modern medicine now knows about leprosy, or Hansen's disease, Scripture scholars suspect leprosy was not all that common in the ancient Middle East. Other skin diseases causing blotches or blemishes, such as eczema or psoriasis, were in all likelihood often misdiagnosed as leprosy. While this would mitigate the physical suffering actually endured by those incorrectly diagnosed, it did nothing to alleviate the mental and psychological anguish they suffered from the religious and social stigmas attendant on those labeled lepers. Even more perniciously, faulty diagnoses swelled the number of innocent victims.

As seen in the first reading, the Book of Leviticus tightly controlled the conduct of lepers. They were to keep their distance from ordinary society and cry out in warning, "Unclean, unclean!", should anyone inadvertently happen to approach them. Fear of contracting leprosy was so deeply ingrained at the time that no one was likely to approach them willingly. In light of the Mosaic Law (Lv 13:45-46) and the common custom of the day, the fact that the leper in today's Gospel dared to approach Jesus at all was a sign of the man's great desperation and his even greater faith.

Life as a leper was deplorable and they yearned to be free. Mark earlier reported Jesus' reputation rapidly spread everywhere throughout the whole of Galilee (1:28). Judging from today's Gospel, one may surmise it reached even the leper colonies. Since the only way out of the leper colony was a cure, for the man to approach Jesus he had to believe Jesus could cure him. And that is exactly what he professes, "If you wish, you can make me clean." Jesus is manifestly touched by his faith. Despite his disease which would cause most people to recoil, Jesus first shows his humanity by reaching out and touching him, thereby acknowledging and accepting him as a fellow human being. Then Jesus manifests his divinity by curing him of the most dreaded disease of the day with a simple command, "I do will it. Be made clean." Since leprosy was considered the worst disease that could befall humankind, and disease was commonly associated in people's minds with sin, the cure of the leper also suggests Jesus has the power to forgive sin. The critical point Mark makes here evolves from an implied comparison. Just as Jesus eliminated the leprosy, restored the leper to physical health, and returned him to human society, so Jesus by his divine power can expunge our sins, reinstate our spiritual wholeness, and reunite us once again to God's love. Immediately after the cure Jesus warns the man to tell no one, something referred to as the Messianic secret. Jesus had come to preach the good news that the kingdom of God was at hand and it was time to repent and reform. His miracles were intended primarily to support his teaching. People often preferred his cures to his call to repentance, however, and Jesus did not want to mislead them. But the man cannot contain himself and blabs all over. As a result, we see a surprising reversal of roles in the first chapter of Mark. The chapter begins with Jesus moving freely from town to town preaching the Gospel, while the leper is isolated in a deserted place. It ends with the leper allowed to move freely about while Jesus is forced to seek refuge in deserted places to avoid the crush of the crowds pressing around him and to find time to pray.

The ancient practice of ostracizing and isolating lepers seems barbaric today. But we do similar things in our own society. Widows often feel cut off from friends. The friends are there at the wake but then soon disappear because no one seems to want an unattached female around. Cancer patients frequently feel neglected because people are uncomfortable with the disease and shy away. Seniors in old age homes complain their families rarely come to visit them. Families of alcoholics speak of being cut off and isolated because no one wants to get involved in a drinking problem.

Amid such widespread insensitivity, even a single individual can often make a significant difference. When one of LBJ's assistants was arrested on a morals charge, his family found itself immediately ostracized in Washington. Knowing that the press dogged her every step, Lady Bird deliberately showed up on their doorstep one day carrying a big bouquet of flowers to counter the cruel trend and show her solidarity with the family. One of John XXIII's first public visits after being elected pope was to Rome's largest prison. He went, knowing Rome's ubiquitous troop of pa-

parazzi would be in hot pursuit, to visit his cousin who was serving a prison sentence. On meeting his cousin, with cameras flashing and microphones poised to catch every sound, he quipped with his typical self-deprecating humor, "Since you couldn't come to see me, I came to see you."

Curing the Paralytic Lowered
Through the Roof

There is more going on in today's Gospel than at first meets the eye. Up until this point in Mark's Gospel Jesus has met with unqualified and unquestioned success as he hastened about preaching, teaching, and healing all manner of illness to the awestruck praise of all he encountered. Shortly before, as we read in last week's Gospel, Jesus had healed a leper whose subsequent unwelcome broadcasting of the cure sent people scurrying to Jesus in droves. The crowds persist even when Jesus returns home, filling the house where he stayed and spilling over outside the door. Four men come carrying a paralyzed friend on a litter in search of a cure but are unable to get near Jesus due to the large crowd. Using their own ingenuity or perhaps urged on by their crippled compatriot, they head for the roof.

To understand what happens next we should recall that houses in Palestine were flat-topped rectangles, much like the Indian pueblos in our southwest. The beams of the roof were crisscrossed or thatched over with palm branches providing both cover and ventilation. There were generally stairs along the outside wall of the house leading to the roof, allowing the residents to sleep under the stars on sweltering nights. With easy access to the roof, all the men had to do was remove some of the branches to let the paralytic down before Jesus. Their faith did the rest. Astounded by the depth of faith motivating this clever maneuver, Jesus spontaneously says to the paralytic in a voice loud enough for all to hear, "Your sins are forgiven."

Recall that at the time sickness and suffering were regarded as punishment for sin (Jn 9:2). The people in the audience were most likely startled by the interruption of the paralytic's dramatic descent into their midst and may have instinctively wondered what sin he had committed to end up paralyzed. In any event, Jesus inverts the usual order of a cure and begins by forgiving the man's sins. The scribes in the group immediately take exception to his words. This unfortunately marks the beginning of a tragic controversy between the religious authorities and Jesus that will continue to fester and intensify through the rest of the Gospel. It culminates sadly at the end of the Gospel when the religious authorities publicly demand the death of Jesus on the very same charge they level in their hearts against him now, blasphemy (Mk 14:63).

Why the strong reaction? Since sin is an offense against God, only God can forgive sin. This is indeed true, so Jesus is claiming more than human power. Jesus will soon back up his claim by curing the paralyzed man miraculously, but the scribes prove unwilling to wait and leap to judgment, in part for personal reasons. Their livelihood as scribes hinged on transcribing and transmitting the law and the prophets to current and future generations. The law prescribed detailed rituals of what had to be done in seeking God's forgiveness, including sacrifices of atonement offered by priests in the Temple. As strict adherents and staunch defenders of the law, scribes would naturally not welcome any diminution of its importance or centrality. This unfortunately seems to have blinded them to the purpose and meaning of Jesus' mission. In claiming divine power for himself, Jesus appeared to be circumventing traditional ways. His powerful intervention on behalf of the physically and spiritually afflicted challenged their role and threatened their niche.

In reporting that Jesus was immediately aware of their thinking, Mark once again imputes divine power to Jesus because only God can judge the human heart (Ps 7:10). In a series of questions Jesus then spells out the essence of the reasoning process that should accompany any miracle. Which is easier to say, "Your sins are forgiven" or "Rise, pick up your mat, and walk"? Since there is no way of offering tangible proof for a cure of a spiritual disorder such as sin, Jesus offers a cure of what was commonly believed to be the result of sin, namely physical illness, which in this case happened to be paralysis. If Jesus can demonstrate greater than merely human power in curing an illness people can see, then people should be ready to take him at his word when he says he can cure them of things they cannot see. Since only God can reverse the effects of sin and overcome or supersede the forces of nature, the miracles demonstrate beyond any reasonable shadow of doubt that Jesus acts with the very power of God. To those who are open-minded and reflective, each miracle also strongly implies that Jesus himself is truly God.

Not all were honest with themselves and God, however, nor willing to challenge themselves and their assumptions. Many ordinary people preferred Jesus' miracles to his message and hoped to bend Jesus and his mission to their political ambitions for national sovereignty and temporal prosperity. Many a scribe and religious leader proved too wedded to the past to give Jesus a fair hearing. As the physical paralysis leaves the man, we sadly witness the beginning of a moral paralysis set in on this type of person.

Today we sometimes wonder how people could have failed to respond to Jesus and his miracles. But God is active in our lives, too, and intervenes with constant miracles that often pass unnoticed: a baby's smile, a glorious sunset, a spouse who understands without a word ever being spoken, a friend there when most needed but least expected, a chance to make a difference. But how often do we recognize God's visitation and gift, how often do we thank him, how often do we praise him? We can well imagine the exhilaration of the paralytic when he could stand up and walk. As paralysis cripples the body, so sin incapacitates the soul. Do we feel the same exhilaration and offer fitting gratitude at being freed from sin?

New Cloth, Old Wineskins

Today's Gospel is part of an escalating conflict between the religious authorities and Jesus. Last week in the cure of the paralytic we read the scribes murmured in their hearts that Jesus blasphemed (Mk 2:7). Then some scribes, who also happened to be Pharisees, challenged Jesus' disciples openly over their master's willing association at table with sinners and tax collectors (Mk 2:16). In today's Gospel some people in the crowd confront Jesus directly for the first time with the challenge, "Why do the disciples of John and the disciples of the Pharisees fast, but your disciples do not fast?"

According to Mosaic Law there was only one day in the year prescribed for fasting, which was Yom Kippur, the Day of Atonement (Lv 16:29). It was a solemn day of repentance for sin, marked by profound sorrow. Public fasts were added later on occasions of national mourning such as the death of Saul and his sons (1 S 31:13) and in time of natural disasters such as plagues of swarming locusts (Jl 1:14). These fasts were also intrinsically associated with occasions of sorrow. Private fasts were a matter of personal devotion, often performed in preparation for an important task or to seek God's aid and forgiveness (Dn 9:3). Jesus fasted forty days before beginning his mission (Mt 4:2); the early Church fasted for special intentions (Ac 13:2, 14:23). Pharisees fasted publicly twice a week, on Mondays and on Thursdays.

In asking why his disciples do not fast, the scribes and Pharisees infer Jesus is lax as a religious leader. Jesus replies in marital imagery, referring to himself as a groom. He asks how the wedding guests can fast while the groom is still with them, conjuring up some of the human heart's happiest memories: those of a wedding feast. In Scripture the kingdom of God is often compared to a bridal banquet because humankind is at its happiest and best when surrounded at table by the family and friends they love. God is also frequently referred to as a bridegroom in the Old Testament. As we see in the first reading from Hosea today, God is the husband; Israel, the bride. With this direct allusion to a wedding feast and himself as groom, Jesus informs his antagonists that the kingdom of God has in fact dawned upon the world in his very person. Since the Jewish people had also come to identify messianic times with the abundance and overflowing typically associated with a wedding banquet, Jesus further suggests he is the Messiah. In light of the good news that the kingdom of God has broken forth and messianic times have arrived, therefore, there can be no time or cause for fasting. Fasting, according to custom, was appropriate in time of sorrow and preparation. With Jesus in their midst issuing in messianic times and establishing the kingdom of God on earth, the present moment calls solely for rejoicing. Only later when he is taken away (a reference to his death), will fasting be an appropriate response, as it was at the death of Saul (1 S 31:13).

Jesus then follows up with two parables about cloth and wineskins, each of which draws a contrast between new and old. Why, people wonder, were these two parables in particular remembered? Scripture scholars reply by referring to the *Sitz in Leben* or situation in the early Church. A pressing problem for early Christians was whether they were obliged to observe the Mosaic Law as well as the Christian law, to follow the old and the new. These parables about old and new helped toward the solution. Jesus had come to fulfill Old Testament law, not to destroy it. But his teaching went so far beyond the Mosaic Law that the old ways often could not keep up. We need cite but a few examples.

Moses had taught an eye for an eye, a tooth for a tooth. He did so to introduce a note of proportionality and curb the excessive vengeance and violence prevalent in his day. When Jewish ethics fully accepted the idea of proportionality, Jesus then invited people to a higher morality: turn the other cheek, walk the extra mile. The Old Testament says love your fellow countrymen. With twelve disparate tribes, that proved difficult at first. The Exodus experience helped to pull the tribes together but it was not until David that all twelve tribes finally united as one nation. When they came to accept each other, Jesus then challenged them a mighty step further: love your enemies, do good to those who hate you. In these and in so many other areas, what Moses began and the Jewish people eventually accepted as normative, Jesus brought to completion, eventually summing up all of the Old Testament law and prophets in the two commandments of perfect love: love of God and love of neighbor. Since all the Old Testament is directed precisely at this goal, Jesus thereby fulfilled the law and prophets. Thus, in fulfilling Jesus' law of perfect love, Christians came to realize they also fulfilled all the essentials of the Mosaic Law.

Jesus and the Pharisees, however, couldn't have been farther apart in their approach to religion. The Pharisees' compulsion for specifics complicated religious observance and led to an endless multiplication of laws and requirements. Jesus, on the other hand, worked to simplify religious practice by identifying basic attitudes that would cover all eventualities. The two approaches were completely incompatible and simply could not coexist, as Jesus explains with the two brief parables in today's Gospel. Both make exactly the same point but, interestingly enough, each is gender-specific, providing corroborating evidence independent of the Lucan tradition that Jesus indeed tailored his stories to the needs of his audience.

The first image is intended for women who in those days were responsible for making and maintaining their families' clothes. Cloth in ancient times did not come preshrunk. If one tried to use new cloth (Jesus' approach) to patch old cloth (the Pharisees' approach), the new cloth would shrink at the first washing and tear the old cloth apart. Every woman in the audience would immediately grasp the folly of the endeavor. The second image is directed at men whose task it was to grow the grapes and make the wine. Wine was fermented and stored in animal skins. New skins were pliable and could withstand the pressure of fermentation. But old skins dried with age, lost their elasticity, and were apt to explode under pressure. No vintner would entrust new wine (Jesus' teaching) to old skins (the Pharisees' tradition), as all the men in the audience would fully understand.

The point of today's Gospel and its two parables, then, is that Jesus came to build, not to destroy. But his message was unfortunately incompatible with the rigid Pharisaical norms common at the time. Let us pray that we not insist that God conform to our ways as the Pharisees did but rather that we always be docile to the Spirit and humbly submit to God's will in every aspect of our lives.

Temptation in the Desert

Today is the First Sunday in Lent. In all three liturgical cycles, the Gospel for the First Sunday in Lent is the Temptation of Jesus in the desert. While Matthew and Luke describe Jesus' struggle with Satan in rich and vivid detail, Mark treats this epic encounter only in passing, as a brief but important transition from the Baptism of Jesus (Mk 1:9) to the beginning of his Public Life (Mk 1:14). Instead Mark chooses to rely on a few key images that were sure to evoke memories of similar past events and invite comparison. Recall that many readers were steeped in the Old Testament because Scripture at the time represented the written repository of all Jewish history, theology, literature, and law. Devoting a scant two lines to the entire episode, Mark tells us little more than the Spirit drove Jesus into the desert to be tempted for forty days. The geographical location (desert) and the duration of time (forty), however, particularly when mentioned in concert, would invariably call to mind earlier individuals and events critical to salvation history.

In 1 Kings 19 we read Elijah fled into the desert to escape the death threats issued against him by Queen Jezebel. She was enraged because he had bested and killed four hundred prophets of Baal, the god she had brought with her from Phoenicia on her marriage to King Ahab of Israel. In the desert Elijah is fed by an angel of God and sent on a forty-day journey without further food to Horeb or Sinai, the same mountain where Moses received the Ten Commandments. God comes to him there under the guise of a gentle wind and commissions him to anoint Jehu the new king of Israel and Elisha as his own successor. The desert and forty days of fasting thus played a vital part in preparing Elijah for his God-given task. The similar setting surrounding today's episode suggests Jesus continues in the noble tradition of the great prophet Elijah and the mission he is about to undertake is of even greater importance.

But the number forty and the desert setting also had far deeper resonances in the Jewish psyche. The pairing of the two would conjure up memories both of Moses, the great leader and liberator of the Jewish people, and of the Exodus itself, the defining moment in Jewish history when Moses led the Hebrews from slavery in Egypt to freedom and sovereignty in the Promised Land. During their wanderings in the desert for forty years, God tested Moses and the people to determine whether they were worthy to be God's chosen people and bear the name of the great patriarch Israel, whom God regarded as his son. Through their many trials and tribulations, by avid intercession with God, Moses was always able to feed his followers with manna from heaven (Ex 16) and provide them with water in an otherwise arid landscape (Nb 20).

The strong similarities yet marked differences between the desert experience of the Jews and that of Jesus invite comparisons between Jesus on the one hand and Moses and the Israelites on the other. Jesus is the new Moses who will lead his people not from physical slavery as in Egypt but from the spiritual slavery of sin, not to the Promised Land of Palestine but to the kingdom of God on earth as a foretaste of heaven. On their journey Jesus will nourish his followers with food for eternal life, with bread and wine that are his body and blood. Scripture also sadly records that in their trek through the desert the Jewish people failed time and again to rise to God's challenges of faith. By contrast, in his desert temptation Jesus obeyed God perfectly in all things, thereby proving he is truly God's Son, the new Israel, the beginning of a new people of God.

Mark ends his brief temptation scene with simply a reference to Jesus being amid wild beasts with angels coming to minister to him. The conclusion is consistent and in keeping with the rest of the scene. It is equally cryptic yet equally pregnant with scriptural symbolism. The image of Jesus living peacefully among wild animals summons up memories of the familiar Genesis account of creation where in their innocence before original sin, Adam and Eve lived at peace with all living things (Gn 1:28). But Adam and

Eve failed in their very first test and fell from grace, destroying the previous harmony that had existed both between God and them and between nature and humankind. In prevailing over Satan and refusing to sin, Jesus is seen as the new Adam, the beginning of a new creation where peace and harmony can once more be established, an amity that was destroyed by the first Adam's sin.

When the all too brief temptation scene ends, Mark reports that Jesus immediately began to preach. In so doing, Mark suggests the desert ordeal was simply a preparation for the public ministry of Jesus. God used Elijah's forty-day trek and trial in the desert to prepare him for an important commission. God took forty years in the desert wilderness to shape the twelve tribes of Israel into a nation of his own special people. Similarly, Jesus set aside forty days of fasting and prayer to prepare for his mission.

The Church asks us to deepen our faith commitment during the forty days of Lent. Fasting and self-denial seem currently out of fashion. We will starve ourselves and follow foolish fad diets to trim our waistlines and improve our figures, but we balk at curbing our appetites or foreswearing some favorite treat for the spiritual gain of better control of our physical drives and desires. While bodily denial can at times be beneficial, it is nevertheless not what the Church stresses in Lent. What the Church urges is control of our hearts, minds, and tongues. As Isaiah (58) directs, it is the curbing of violence and injustice, concern for the homeless and the hungry, that God desires. These are areas we can all work to improve during Lent. We can also pay greater attention to weekday Mass, daily prayer, greater charity at home and at work, volunteer service, visiting the elderly and sick, and almsgiving.

The Transfiguration

As with many of the key events in the life of Jesus, when we read the Gospel account of the Transfiguration we need to distinguish between (1) what the Apostles actually perceived at the time of the event and (2) what they and the early Church understood of the event after the death and resurrection of Jesus. Mark states the Apostles were "terrified" (Mk 9:6), suggesting they were more than a little befuddled at the time and not fully cognizant of all that was transpiring. The subsequent careful and loving recording of each detail of the event, however, reflects the Church's post-resurrection awareness of the rich significance of the episode, and it is from this perspective that the passage is best examined.

The Transfiguration is central to Mark's Gospel. He clearly wrote his account to show Jesus is the Son of God. At three critical junctures in the Gospel he reports it boldly: at the Baptism of Jesus in the very beginning of the Gospel (Mk 1:11), at the crucifixion near the end of the Gospel (Mk 15:39), and here at the Transfiguration which is the mid-point of his Gospel (Mk 9:7).

Mark is also careful to give us the background for the Transfiguration. It is set at a time when Jesus was preparing his disciples for his passion and death. Six days before he had warned them for the first time that he had to suffer and die and after three days rise again and that they too also had to take up their crosses and follow him (Mk 8:31-38). But they proved both unwilling and unable to grasp his message, particularly what he meant by rising again, so Jesus promises that some of them would not taste death until they see the kingdom of God come in power (Mk 9:1).

At the Transfiguration, six days later, Peter, James, and John see Jesus grow radiant in the company of Moses and Elijah. In some Jewish circles Moses and Elijah were thought to have escaped the effects of death. Elijah was reported to have been taken up into heaven in a fiery chariot (2 K 2:11). Deuteronomy (34:5-7) records that Moses died but no one knows where he was buried and that to the very end of his life his eyes remained undimmed, his vigor unabated. From this text pious Jews surmised Moses never tasted death like other mortals and belief in the Assumption of Moses sprung up. The appearance of these two figures in particular, then, is dramatic confirmation of God's power to bestow life after death, the very thing Jesus had told his disciples of earlier, yet which few Jews, even the Apostles, dared accept or dream possible.

In revelation history God's presence is often denoted by a cloud. A cloud led the Jewish people through the desert during the Exodus (Ex 13:21). A cloud covered Mt. Sinai when God gave the Commandments to Moses (Ex 19:16). A cloud overshadowed the tent of meeting whenever God came to converse with Moses (Ex 33:7-10). A cloud filled the Holy of Holies when Solomon completed the Temple (1 K 8:10). Here the descent of a cloud at the end of the vision previews the coming of the kingdom of God on earth for the three Apostles standing there, fulfilling Jesus' earlier prophecy that some would not taste death until they had seen God's kingdom come in power. Yet far greater proof still lay ahead for them and the early Church in the resurrection of Jesus.

God intended the Transfiguration to fortify the Apostles for Gethsemane and Golgotha, to strengthen them for the passion and death of Jesus, and to help them survive with faith intact when the forces of evil were given sway and allowed their way with Jesus on Good Friday. God also designed it, however, to help the Apostles and the early Church understand the pivotal role of Jesus in salvation history. In the vision Jesus appears with Moses and Elijah. Moses was considered the greatest lawgiver in the Old Testament. The Mosaic Law, which bears his name, codified both the religious and civil law of the Jewish people throughout biblical times. Elijah, a particularly charismatic prophet, was popularly regarded as preeminent among the prophets. In this vision, Moses clearly personifies the law; Elijah, the prophets. And up until this point in time, the two major sources of revelation were precisely the Law and the Prophets.

Before he died Moses had promised God would send a prophet like himself to whom the people should listen (Dt 18:15). Malachi had also promised God would send Elijah before the Day of the Lord to set people's hearts straight (Ml 3:23). Now as the vision draws to a close, Moses and Elijah, representing the Law and the Prophets, disappear. Jesus stands alone beneath the cloud and God's voice declares, "Listen to him." The unmistakable meaning is that from this point on Jesus is the sole source of revelation. He supersedes the Law and the Prophets. For the early Church, many of whom were Jewish and concerned about their obligation to fulfill the Mosaic Law, this solved a pressing problem. In following Jesus, they would fulfill all of the Law and the Prophets. Henceforth, they had only to look to Jesus.

I can't conclude without a word about the first reading from Genesis. The story of Abraham sacrificing Isaac is one of the most disturbing in all of Scripture. Recall that child sacrifice was common at the time. People felt they had to offer God what was most dear, and what could be dearer than one's firstborn child? Through his willingness to offer God whatever he wanted, Abraham clearly demonstrated God came first in his life. In refusing to allow Abraham's sacrifice of Isaac, God showed unmistakably he did not want human sacrifice. Rather, God wants the wholehearted dedication of our lives and selves. The story of Abraham was crucial in showing the Jewish people that the practice of child sacrifice was pagan and wrong. Equally important, it shows us today, by way of contrast, how much God loves the world. He who would not accept Abraham's sacrifice of his son, Isaac, did not hesitate to sacrifice his only Son to save humankind from sin.

Cleansing of the Temple

To understand today's Gospel and Jesus' undeniable wrath, we must first understand something of the layout of the Temple. The Temple was surrounded by massive walls not only to forestall invasion but also to segregate the hallowed space within from the noises, smells, and dust of the city and its markets outside the gates. The walls were purposely designed as a buffer between the sacred and the secular. Immediately inside the gate was an open area called the Court of the Gentiles, accessible to Jew and pagan alike. Within the outer walls and initial main courtyard was a series of inner walls and courtyards leading to progressively more sacred space. First came the Court of Women where the Treasury was located, then came the Court of Men where the altar of sacrifice was situated. Both areas were off limits to all but Jews. In the deepest interior lay the Holy of Holies, the very dwelling place of God on earth.

Ideally, by architect's design, on entering the main gate one would experience a sense of peace on leaving the hustle and bustle of the throbbing metropolis outside and feel drawn by the tranquility and calm of the courtyard to grow prayerful in proximity to God's abiding presence. Instead, Jesus was jarred by the shouts of moneychangers touting their rates and the braying of livestock awaiting sale. What were moneychangers and livestock vendors doing within the sacred space of the Temple itself?

John tells us it was Passover time. By Jewish law every adult male living within a fifteen-mile radius of Jerusalem was bound to attend Temple services. Many Jews from all over the world also came out of devotion, much as Moslems flock to Mecca today for the *Hajj.* As a result, Passover saw Jerusalem filled to overflowing with Jews from around the globe. On coming to the Temple, they had to pay a Temple tax for the upkeep and support of the buildings and services. Temple authorities, the priestly aristocracy known as the Sadducees, required the tax be paid in Jewish currency because other currencies bore images of foreign rulers and this was deemed idolatry by pious Jews. Temple officials thus profited handsomely by exchanging Jewish coinage, which was all but worthless outside the Temple and rarely used in commerce, for hard currency, such as Roman currency, which was internationally accepted and widely used by all but the most observant Jews. The moneychangers were in the Temple precincts, therefore, to facilitate the necessary exchange of currencies. They did so for a fee, of course, which was generally considered exorbitant. As a result, Jewish moneychangers were called the equivalent of Shylock in English.

Pilgrims also came to the Temple to offer sacrifice. Jewish law demanded all sacrificial animals be without defect (Lv 22:17-21). Temple inspectors were there to check. They were known, however, to favor animals purchased in the Temple over animals brought in from outside where prices were considerably lower. This created a virtual monopoly for the approved dealers inside the Temple precincts. Pilgrims to Jerusalem with limited time to spend could not risk the chance of an animal being rejected and so had to buy from the Temple market to be safe. This in turn enabled authorities to charge higher fees to support the Temple but it all came out of the pilgrim's pocket in the end. While lucrative for Temple authorities and activities, the animal market mucked up the main courtyard of the Temple, befouled the air, created a din, and wreaked havoc with the prayerful, peaceful atmosphere that by right should have prevailed within the Temple. Justifiably angry at the cacophony confronting him on entering the Temple, Jesus vents his ire at the crassness of the moneychangers, the brashness of the animal vendors, and the greed of the Temple officials.

In his manifest unhappiness with Temple policy and services, Jesus took his place in a long line of prophets such as Hosea (6:6, 8:11) and Jeremiah (7:13-23). More importantly, the drama of Jesus' driving the moneychangers and animal vendors out of the Temple bore unmistakable messianic overtones. Malachi had foretold the coming of the Messiah in terms of God sending his messenger who would suddenly enter the Temple and purify the sons of Levi (priests) so that acceptable offerings could be made (Ml 3:1-4). The Temple officials recognized at once the significance of Jesus' action and immediately challenged his authority by asking for a sign. The Jews regarded the Temple itself as a sign of God's presence, so Jesus uses allegory to indicate that he himself is the sign.

Allegory is a form of speech that employs imagery to communicate on more than one level. Referring to the temple of his body, Jesus replies, "Destroy this temple and in three days I will raise it up." The Temple officials scoff at his reply, thinking he is talking about the Temple that surrounds them. The first Temple built by Solomon was destroyed by the Babylonians in 587 BC. The second Temple built by Zerubbabel after the Babylonian exile was dedicated in 515 BC and remained largely unchanged until Herod the Great began major reconstruction in 19 BC. The bulk of the reconstruction was completed in ten years but embellishments continued well into the time of Jesus. Officials tallied it took 46 years in all. But Jesus was speaking not of this massive stone structure but of his body. And the sign of his authority from God which he alludes to will be his resurrection from the dead, which was God's ultimate seal of approval.

Jesus ended up driving the animals out of the Temple. Besides the practical purpose of this endeavor, it had symbolic meaning. In light of his upcoming death and resurrection, there would be no more need for animal sacrifice. Jesus had earlier told the Samaritan woman that a day was coming when people would worship not at a temple but in spirit and truth (Jn 4:21-23). As Christians, we now pray in and through the risen Jesus wherever we happen to be.

Being Lifted Up

Today's Gospel from John is difficult but important. It is difficult because it uses symbols to reflect back on the Old Testament while at the same time projecting forward into the New Testament. It is important because it contains two verses that are generally regarded as the most successful in summing up the whole Gospel message.

Let us start by looking back into the Old Testament. In Numbers we read that once freed from the tyranny of Egyptian domination, while wandering through the Sinai at the time of the Exodus, the Jewish people complained often and bitterly about conditions in the desert, particularly the monotony of the manna from heaven. They longed by way of contrast for the fleshpots of Egypt where, though enslaved in deplorable conditions, they had savored and enjoyed fresh fish, meat, cucumbers, melons, leeks, onions, and garlic (Nb 11:5-6).

Despite repeatedly witnessing God's saving power and personal intervention on their behalf, they remained sullenly unsatisfied and stubbornly unconvinced of God's all-caring and loving providence. So God punished them by allowing saraph serpents to penetrate the perimeter of their camp with their fatal and painful bite. The Jewish people belatedly realized they had offended God by their lack of faith and asked for forgiveness. God relented and directed Moses to mount a bronze replica of the serpent on a pole. Anyone looking on the bronze figure with faith would be saved (Nb 21:4-9). The image of a serpent mounted on a pole perdures to this day. Centuries ago the medical profession adopted the figure as the symbol for medicine. Known as a caduceus, it is frequently seen on prescription forms and at pharmacy counters.

In today's Gospel John uses this familiar caduceus symbol from the Old Testament to predict for the very first time the crucifixion of Jesus. He tells us, "And just as Moses lifted up the serpent in the desert, so must the Son of Man be lifted up that everyone who believes in him may have eternal life." John thereby implies that anyone who looks on Jesus mounted on the pole of the cross with faith will be saved. But whereas the bronze serpent merely restored physical health, the crucified Jesus would restore spiritual wholeness leading to eternal life. John thus uses Old Testament imagery to foreshadow what will be the central event in New Testament history.

With the caduceus image John reveals a personal insight that reflects his own unique theological perspective. The verb "to lift up" or "to mount" in both Numbers and in John carries the distinct connotation of "to exalt." Alone among the evangelists, John consistently maintains a post-resurrection viewpoint. He sees and interprets all the events in the life of Jesus in light of the resurrection, which was God's ultimate and supreme exaltation of Jesus. Consequently, in predicting the passion and death of Jesus, John refers to Jesus as being lifted up on the cross in the sense of being exalted on the cross, just as three days later Jesus would be raised up and exalted in the resurrection. For John, the crucifixion and resurrection are inexorably linked as inseparable parts of a whole or as seamless sections of the same garment. For John with his post-resurrection viewpoint, Jesus was glorified on the cross, not humiliated, since the cross was simply the prelude to the resurrection. Similarly, the crucifixion was not a defeat but a victory because it succeeded ultimately in destroying the power of evil and reuniting humankind once again with God.

John next proffers the reason for the death and resurrection of Jesus in two succinct but critically important verses that Scripture scholars say summarize the whole of the Gospel message: "For God so loved the world that he gave his only Son, so that everyone who believes in him might not die but might have eternal life. For God did not send his Son into the world to condemn the world, but that the world might be saved through him" (Jn 3:16-17). This is the Good News that the Apostles were enjoined to teach. Remember the original and literal translation of "Gospel" is simply "Good News." If asked to sum up all of the Gospel in two lines, therefore, we can do no better than repeat these two lines from John (3:16-17).

The Good News, then, is that God seeks not to condemn us but to save us. This reveals another key facet of John's thinking. In John's theology God condemns no one. It is we who condemn ourselves, but only if we fail to accept God's Son and receive him into our lives with faith. John then proceeds to develop the idea with his favorite image of light and darkness. Jesus is the light of the world, the light by which we can see and judge things correctly, i.e., as God sees and judges them. Those who live and direct their lives in the light of Jesus' teaching will have everlasting life. Those who refuse the illumination of Jesus' teaching and example, preferring the darkness of their own selfishness, shallowness, and sin, on the other hand, condemn themselves for not accepting Jesus and his truth. They are like anorexics who deny their bodies good food in order to nurture a sick and distorted self-image that will eventually kill them.

Besides providing the most comprehensive summary of the Gospel, the two verses in John (3:16-17) also offer the proper perspective on salvation history. Too often we have it all backwards and think everything depends on us. We feel we have to do something to merit God's love. If we are good, then God will love us. If we are bad, then God will not or cannot love us. We think it not only depends on us but also begins with us. But the Gospel today tells us just the opposite. The initiative for all salvation comes from God and God alone. It is he who loves us first and who personally looks out for each one of us and our eternal well-being. For even when the world was steeped in sin, God did not hesitate to send his only Son to save us.

The Son of Man Must be Glorified

Today's Gospel passage from John takes place at Passover time when Jews from all over the world came to Jerusalem to celebrate the feast. Passover was universally considered the most important feast of the year. One of three pilgrimage feasts, along with Pentecost and Tabernacles, it was a time when all Jews in reasonable proximity to Jerusalem were required to attend Temple services and Jews everywhere else were encouraged to join the commemoration in Zion whenever they could. Passover was originally a family feast celebrated locally. It became a pilgrimage feast only after the reforms of Josiah when the codes of Deuteronomy (12:1-7) were at last implemented, abolishing all the local shrines and restricting all animal sacrifice to the Temple in Jerusalem. The change is reported in the Second Book of Kings (23:21-23) as taking place in the eighteenth year of Josiah's reign, which would be 621 BC.

John tells us some Greeks came to see Jesus. They may have been proselytes, people seriously thinking of converting to Judaism. Or they may have simply been merchants trying to profit from the vast throng of tourists who had flocked to Jerusalem with money in their pockets to celebrate the high holy days. Somehow these Greeks had heard of Jesus and his message and had come to seek him out. Mention of them supports John's earlier claim that many were coming over to Jesus (8:30) and lays the groundwork for Jesus' later assertion that he would draw all people to himself (12:32).

The Greeks approach Philip who had a Greek name and was from Bethsaida on the northeast shore of the Sea of Galilee near the region of the Decapolis with its ten Hellenistic cities. Philip may have been familiar with Greeks and even been able to speak some Greek from having lived near the border of a Greek-speaking region. He had earlier brought Nathanael to Jesus (Jn 1:45). Now he brings the Greeks to Andrew who also had a Greek name and hailed from the same region. Andrew had a wonderful way of introducing people to Jesus. Early on he had introduced his brother Simon to Jesus (Jn 1:41) and later the boy with the five barley loaves and two fish that were to provide the wherewithal for the multiplication of loaves and fish (Jn 6:8-9). Now we see him introducing the Greek travelers.

When Jesus hears about the Greeks, who are Gentiles, he declares, "The hour has come for the Son of Man to be glorified." The Son of Man here is a title borrowed from the Book of Daniel. Daniel had characterized the four latest superpowers to rule the world, i.e., the Babylonians, Medes, Persians, and Greeks, as so savage and barbaric that they could only be described as animals. The Babylonians he portrayed as a lion, the Medes as a bear, the Persians as a leopard, and the Greeks as a wild beast with iron teeth and ten horns. As a prophet, he then foretold that the wild beast with the iron teeth, the last and worst of all, would be destroyed and the other beasts stripped of their power. Finally a son of man was to appear on the clouds and receive sovereignty over all the world. This son of man would ultimately issue in a new kingdom that would be humane, peaceful, God-fearing—a kingdom ruled not by a beast but by a son of man (Dn 7). With the dominion of this figure over all the superpowers of the world, a universal note is added to the future coming of the reign of God, suggesting God's kingdom will be open to all, even the Gentiles.

From the Book of Daniel onward the Jews looked forward to the coming of the son of man as the Messiah, the one who would issue in a new kingdom and drive out all foreign powers. This reinforced their expectation that the Messiah would be a powerful political figure and mighty warrior. So when Jesus moves from the son of man being glorified to a grain of wheat dying, they are confused and walk away. Many Jews and a good number of the early disciples could not accept the notion of a suffering Messiah, even though it was part and parcel of the tradition as evidenced by the Suffering Servant Songs of Isaiah (42, 49, 50, 52). They wanted to hear nothing about hating one's life to save it or serving others as a servant serves a master. The thought of laying down one's life to produce fruit or save others was also abhorrent to them. Yet Jesus accepted death because dying is an integral though painful part of being human and it enabled him to demonstrate beyond a shadow of a doubt his love for his Father and his complete submission to God's will. As foretold here, his death would bear much fruit, destroying the power of sin and death once and for all by reconciling humankind once again with God and restoring the possibility of life with God forever.

Today's Gospel contains John's account of the Agony in the Garden. While the other three Gospel accounts all tell of Jesus undergoing unspeakable mental anguish, so intense as to cause his body to break out in a bloody sweat, John mentions nothing at all about suffering or doubt. This follows from the theological perspective he adopts throughout his Gospel. As mentioned last week, John views the entire life of Jesus from a post-resurrection viewpoint. For John the suffering and death of Jesus were simply a prelude to the resurrection, an inseparable part of the same fabric, in which the suffering and death, as horrible as they were, are swallowed up and overwhelmed by the glory and exaltation of his being raised up in a new and glorified body to live forever at God's right hand. Consequently, John merely mentions Jesus' human doubt, "I am troubled now," and moves immediately to his fatal but world-saving decision to submit to God's will completely: "But it was for this purpose I came to this hour. Father, glorify your name."

The hour of which Jesus speaks is the time of his death and resurrection, the time when he will be glorified for perfectly fulfilling his Father's will. It will also mark a time of decision and judgment for the world. From that moment on all the people of the world will be called upon to decide whether they will accept or reject Jesus and his saving grace in their lives.

The Passion of the Lord

Today is Passion (Palm) Sunday, the Sunday of the year that the Church has us read the full passion narrative of Our Lord, Jesus Christ. This year in Cycle B we read Mark's Gospel account. Since Mark's passion narrative closely parallels Matthew's and we commented on Matthew's account in detail last year, today let us consider how the passion narrative developed and took shape over time.

The death and resurrection of Jesus are undisputedly the oldest components of the Christian tradition to be handed down. The early Church correctly identified and universally considered them to be the central events in the life of Jesus. While Mark was the first Gospel written, it is not the earliest part of the New Testament. That honor goes to Paul. To trace the development of the passion narrative, therefore, we must start with the epistles of Paul.

In one of his earliest letters, Paul records the nucleus of the original teaching he had been taught and had passed on. In his First Letter to the Corinthians, Paul reports "that Christ died for our sins in accordance with the scriptures; that he was buried; that he was raised on the third day in accordance with the scriptures; that he appeared to Kephas, then to the Twelve" (15: 3-5). This represents the earliest tradition and it is clearly but startlingly bare-boned. Paul immediately adds several post-resurrection appearance accounts. He tells us that Jesus appeared to more than five hundred brothers at once, next to James, then to all the Apostles, and lastly to Paul himself (15:6-8). He provides no specifics or further details about Jesus' passion and death, however. The early Church, as reflected in Paul's epistles, was evidently more concerned with Jesus' resurrection and its aftermath than with his physical sufferings.

Over time, however, people naturally wanted to know more about Jesus. The details of his passion and death were considered among the most important and so were among the first to be filled in, followed by information on his public life and teaching, and lastly by the circumstances of his birth. By the time the Gospels were finally written down, two different strains of the passion account had evolved. The first, reflected in Matthew and Mark, was organized around the fulfillment of Old Testament texts such as the Psalms and the Suffering Servant Songs of Isaiah; the second, adopted by Luke and John, emphasized the words spoken by Jesus, particularly at the Last Supper. The difference between the two can best be seen by comparing the Last Supper accounts of the four evangelists. While Mark and Matthew offer only a few lines about Jesus' final paschal meal with his disciples and portray Jesus as saying very little there, Luke and John build their entire passion narratives around the Last Supper, with John in particular devoting four whole chapters to what Jesus said there while at table.

Sprung from the same strain of the tradition, Matthew and Mark's passion narratives naturally parallel each other closely. With Matthew's account the subject of last year's commentary, we pause here merely to add a word about Mark's opening. Mark begins his passion narrative by exposing a conspiracy. He warns straightaway that the chief priests and scribes were plotting to put Jesus to death. They had plenty of motivation. Jesus had bested them in every test of wits they engaged him in and turned the tables on them in every trap they set for him. He unmasked the hypocrisy that cloaked much of their public and private behavior and refused to conform to the norms they had arbitrarily set for religious leaders. He reviled the shallowness of the Temple rituals that supported the priestly class and the hollowness of the laws which the scribes made their livings legislating and interpreting.

Many members of the Sanhedrin also happened to be clandestine collaborators of Rome who eagerly cooperated with the Romans out of personal and nationalistic interests. Personally they profited from the prominent positions they held, positions that would not be open to them had they not enjoyed Rome's support. Nationalistically, their cooperation with Rome afforded the Jewish people a modicum of independence in strictly internal matters, or so they alleged. They feared that the ordinary people, who chafed under Roman rule, would rise up around Jesus as Messiah and revolt against Rome with disastrous consequences for them and the nation. Hence their perceived need to plot against Jesus to save the nation (Jn 11:49-50).

Since today also happens to be Palm Sunday, let us end with some remarks on the background of this event in Mark (11:1-11), which is read at the Blessing of Palms. According to Mark's account Jesus sensed a groundswell of popular support and accurately anticipated the crowd's reaction as he prepared to enter the Holy City for his last Passover feast. Realizing the likelihood they would welcome him as Messiah and king, Jesus determined to make clear the type of leader he came to be. Many of the Jewish people were hoping for a Messiah who would be politically powerful and militarily mighty, one commanding the most modern army at the time consisting of horses, chariots, and cavalrymen. To counter that image, Jesus deliberately sends for a young donkey to fulfill Zechariah's messianic prophecy: "See, your king shall come to you; a just savior is he, meek and riding on an ass, on a colt, the foal of an ass. He shall banish the chariot from Ephraim, and the horse from Jerusalem; the warrior's bow will be banished, and he will proclaim peace to the nations" (9:9-10).

Jesus' intended symbolism of a meek Messiah escapes the crowd completely, including the Apostles, who will not grasp its significance until after the resurrection. Overcome with joy, people spread their cloaks on the ground before Jesus, as was the custom when a new king ascended the throne. Others cut down branches to honor him as the people did two hundred years before to celebrate their liberation from Antiochus IV under the Maccabees (2 M 10:7). Together they cried, "Hosanna!" and chanted from Psalm 118:26: "Blessed is he who comes in the name of the Lord." Psalm 118 was sung annually on the Feast of Tabernacles, a feast which celebrated Yahweh's kingship and enthronement. It was also the psalm they sang to greet kings and conquering heroes on their return from successful military campaigns and victories in battle. The whole scene, as Mark portrays it, is filled with messianic overtones accurately expressing the people's expectations of Jesus at the moment. While correct in the overall title, they were nonetheless far from the mark with regard to the specifics of what the Messiah involved, and this unfortunately would lead to tragic consequences for all.

The Resurrection

Today's Gospel account of the resurrection of Jesus comes from the Gospel of John. John clearly patterns his account of the first Easter Sunday morning on the beautiful creation story in Genesis that opens the Bible narrative. He does so, consciously and deliberately, to suggest the resurrection marks the beginning of a new creation, a totally new world order in which humankind will henceforth enjoy a completely different relationship with God.

Note the many parallels between John's account of the resurrection and the account of creation in Genesis. John tells us it was "the first day of the week," the day on which God began creation. It was "still dark" when Mary Magdalene came to the tomb, just as "darkness covered the abyss" when God began to create the universe (Gn 1:2). Today's Gospel is set in a garden. The Lord God had planted a garden in Eden (Gn 2:8). As no one was around to witness the resurrection, so no one was present to witness creation. Mary Magdalene arrived after Jesus had risen; Adam and Eve were created only after all else was finished.

The similarities are striking. John uses them to suggest that the death and resurrection of Jesus have issued in a new and higher form of creation. Humankind, now fully reconciled with God and no longer alienated from him by sin, has been raised in status from creatures of God to children of God. As the Israelites' firstborn were spared God's wrath in the plagues of Egypt by the sprinkling of the blood of the Passover lamb on the lintels and door posts of their homes, so those who believe in Jesus are delivered from the effects of sin by the blood of Christ, the new Passover Lamb. Having saved us from sin by his death, Jesus also opens for us through his own resurrection the possibility of our once again enjoying eternal life with God the Father. In John's view of the world, the resurrection raises all creation to new life and possibilities.

In today's passage John also continues to build on the contrast between light and darkness he has developed through much of his Gospel. Darkness is the symbol of evil. It represents the power of Satan and sin in the world. In contrast, Jesus is the light of the world, the true light that illuminates God's ways and enables people to see and understand things as God intends. Throughout his Gospel John pursues the contrast between light and darkness on three different levels: physical, intellectual, and spiritual. On the physical level there is tension between being able to see and not being able to see: *sight* and *blindness*. On the intellectual level the contrast is between *understanding* and *ignorance* because seeing with the mind is equivalent to understanding and not seeing implies ignorance. On the spiritual level where we see with the eyes of the soul, the contrast is between *belief* and *disbelief*. In today's Gospel John masterfully brings all three levels into play.

While the other evangelists all report Mary came at dawn to the empty tomb, John stresses it was still dark, in part to emphasize that Jesus, the Light of the world, had not yet appeared to dispel the darkness engulfing the disciples. It must have been light enough to see because Mary could tell the stone had been rolled back. But she still remains very much in the dark because she immediately jumps to the wrong conclusion. Overwhelmed with the grief of Good Friday, she completely forgets Jesus had three times predicted his resurrection and concludes someone has stolen the body. The darkness of her misgivings will not be dissipated until Jesus later enlightens her by personally appearing to her in the garden. She must see Jesus physically before coming to understand and believe in his resurrection.

Mary meanwhile runs to seek the help of the Apostles. They too are completely in the dark, having failed to understand and thus quickly forgotten Jesus' promise of the resurrection. Peter and the beloved disciple, whom tradition long took to be John, dash off to the tomb. John, who was younger, gets there first but waits out of deference to Peter. He merely peers inside and sees the burial shroud lying on the ground. This provides him with food for thought as Peter arrives and barges headlong into the tomb. Peter sees the entombment wrappings lying separately from the cloth that had covered Jesus' head but light doesn't dawn about its significance. At scene's end he remains as much in the dark as ever. He has seen with his eyes but not understood with his mind or yet believed in his heart.

Next it is John's turn to enter the burial chamber. With his memory jogged from his initial glimpse into the cave and having had time to reflect on things past and present while Peter was inside sizing up the tomb, John views the situation in a new light the second time around and becomes the first one to accept the resurrection. The Gospel tells us, "He saw and believed." Having seen the first time with the eyes of his body and had time to reflect on it, the second time he sees more deeply, with the eyes of his intellect, and draws the correct conclusion. That knowledge then helps him to see with the eyes of the soul and make an act of faith. John becomes the first one to believe in the resurrection. He is the first recorded Christian believer.

So today as we celebrate the Feast of the Resurrection let us recall that in raising Jesus to new life God has also offered us the hope of everlasting life and happiness with him. We should be grateful for his largesse and remember that he also calls us to a new and better life on earth. Through the grace of the death and resurrection of Jesus we are to die to our old sinful ways and live more fully as God's children.

Doubting Thomas

The Church has long considered today's Gospel extremely important. How can we tell? First of all we know the early Church held it in extremely high regard because of the prominent role it is given in the critically important post-resurrection appearances of Jesus. It was clearly cherished, burnished, and often repeated in the Church's teaching and oral tradition prior to the written Gospel account. Two things also tell us it continues to be highly esteemed in the modern Church. For one thing, the Church has us read this particular passage in all three of the liturgical cycles. While this at first may not seem startling, it is in fact highly unusual for the Church to repeat a particular Gospel passage from cycle to cycle. Save for major events in the life of Jesus, like Christmas or Easter, the Church rarely repeats a Gospel passage within a given three-year cycle. When it does so, as today, it obviously considers the message vital. Second, the position assigned the passage, immediately after Easter Sunday, also testifies to its importance. Much as the person to the right of the monarch at a formal dinner party enjoys the second highest place of honor, so the Sunday immediately following Easter receives special preeminence. With Easter the most important feast in the whole liturgical year, the honor of following on its heels lends luster to this particular passage.

The reason this Gospel is so important is that Thomas is a particularly appealing character to whom people can easily relate and with whom they readily sympathize. Yet at the same time he is terribly misguided, in ways people often fail to understand. The combination poses a serious threat to believers and the apostolic ministry of the Church. Uncorrected or unexposed, there is always the danger of his folly leading others inadvertently into the error of his ways.

Thomas, like many a hero of old and many a modern man

and woman today, was a person of strong emotions and close bondings, with a strong sense of self, self-reliance, and self-confidence. He was clearly devoted to Jesus and cocksure he would stand by him through thick and thin. Recall that when Jesus said he had to return to Judea, where people had recently tried to stone him, it was Thomas who prodded the Apostles to accompany him with the somber challenge, "Let us also go to die with him" (Jn 11:16). When Jesus was arrested by the mob, however, Thomas panicked and fled like the rest. As a result, he was devastated. He felt he had failed Jesus and, equally traumatic to Thomas' self-esteem, he had failed himself.

Thomas' perduring appeal to the world, ancient as well as modern, also stems in part from his Stoicism. Having failed his friend and Lord by turning on his heels and leaving him in his hour of need, he was willing to accept what he deemed he deserved. He felt his failure was unforgivable and would not ask for pardon, even though it meant the loss of Jesus' friendship, which crushed him. He was a bighearted man, hard on himself, soft on others. When Jesus appeared to the other Apostles in his absence, he could readily understand how Jesus could forgive them and welcome them back into the fold as if nothing had happened. It was only his weakness, his treachery, his failing that was too egregious to overlook or forgive. It seemed to his exaggerated sense of guilt that Jesus had deliberately and justifiably chosen a time when he was absent to reconcile with the other Apostles. In his heart he longed so much to be reconciled with Jesus that, like a person who can't believe he has won a major lottery, Thomas simply couldn't accept the possibility of Jesus ever forgiving him.

Thomas' faults were two. First was an inflated, albeit perverted, sense of his own self-importance, believing his failure was so unique that not even God could forgive it. Such an attitude belittles God and his mercy, portraying him as little more magnanimous than his creatures. Though common in modern fiction and generally admired as noble, it expresses far more hubris than humility.

It judges God in terms of human standards and expectations and so is completely unworthy of God. Jesus died to forgive all sin and anyone who is truly sorry can return to God with full assurance of complete and absolute forgiveness, no matter how many or great the sins. Isaiah realized this in his day and proclaimed forgiveness was possible even for the likes of Sodom and Gomorrah (Is 1:10, 18).

Second, and far more damaging to the body politic, was Thomas' insistence on direct, personal experience of the risen Jesus. "Unless I see the mark of the nails in his hands ... and put my hand into his side, I will not believe." In asking for signs as the Hebrews did unremittingly all during the Exodus, he exhibited a deplorable lack of faith. Worse, in refusing to believe the Apostles and their eyewitness accounts of the risen Lord, he set the worst possible example for the Church. Consequently, he is pilloried here as the antithesis of what a Christian should be. For, with the ascension of Jesus only forty days away, future believers would have no direct experience of Jesus and would have to rely solely on the testimony of others traced back to the original disciples. To stress the importance of having the proper Christian attitude, John concludes the incident with the only beatitude of Jesus he records in his Gospel: "Blessed are those who have not seen and yet have believed."

The reason today's Gospel is read in all three years of the liturgical cycles, then, is to expose the error of Thomas' ways and warn Christians against self-aggrandizing reliance on one's own initiative. We are rather to trust in God's limitless love for us and accept in faith the testimony of those who have gone before us.

The Road to Emmaus

Today's Gospel starts with a reference to the two disciples of Emmaus and moves on to Jesus visiting the Apostles to strengthen their faith. Both episodes have much in common. The Emmaus tale tells of two disciples of Jesus leaving Jerusalem on Easter Sunday, downcast and discouraged over the crucifixion and death of Jesus. Despite the fact that Jesus had three times predicted his passion, death, and resurrection, they, like everyone else in the early Church, never thought for a moment that Jesus might actually have risen. Not even the testimony of the women who reported an empty grave on Easter morning nor confirmation of the accuracy of their claim by two Apostles gave them pause to believe or hope that Jesus might in fact have risen (Lk 24:22-24). Their departure from Jerusalem was clear indication they believed it was all over.

On their journey home to Emmaus they meet Jesus but do not recognize him. It seems strange that the two who had followed Jesus closely in life would not recognize him after death. But Emmaus is to the west of Jerusalem so they may have had the sun in their eyes as they walked along. More importantly they had never truly recognized him or the true nature of his mission during his life. Like most people, they wanted and expected a powerful Messiah, one who would free them from their bondage to Rome. The word, "Messiah," which is translated "Christ," means "the Anointed One," and all the other important anointed instruments of God's saving power in Old Testament history were strong military or political figures like David, Saul, or Samuel. These early figures had overcome Israel's enemies and set Israel free. Jesus had, for all appearances, however, been vanquished by the Romans, his manner of death a scandal. How could a Messiah sent by God fail in his mission and die such an ignominious death?

In what has been called the most famous Bible lesson in

history, Jesus patiently begins to unfold the meaning of Scripture for them. The Jewish people believed that God communicated to them through Scripture. Though written hundreds of years earlier, Scripture was God's living word that spoke to them in the present and had meaning for current events. Jesus thus helped the disciples to see his life in terms of Scripture and to uncover hidden dimensions of Scripture in terms of his life. In short, he used Old Testament passages to explain New Testament events. Far from promising a political or powerful Messiah, for example, Isaiah in his Suffering Servant Songs spoke of a Messiah who would atone for the sins of all by his personal sufferings. His task was not to free Israel from Rome, but all humankind from sin. Consequently, what happened on Calvary did not signal the failure of his mission, but its fulfillment. Through Scripture, Jesus opened their minds to the meaning of the cross and the reality of the resurrection.

For the two disciples of Emmaus, it was the most important journey of their lives. They thought they knew Jesus, but they came to realize they were far wide of the mark. God's plan far outstripped their expectations. The life of a Christian is also a journey in which we get to know Jesus. Our perceptions also change along the way. For some it comes as a sudden illumination, as for St. Paul on the road to Damascus (Ac 9:1-30). For most, however, it takes a lifetime of deepening awareness. Just as we don't appreciate much in life until we get older—our parents, relatives, acts of kindness and sacrifice made on our behalf—so we frequently fail to appreciate our faith. There is much, for instance, we don't understand of the love of God and his mercy until we have loved, been hurt, and have had to forgive someone in our own lives. Also, how can we appreciate the love of God the Father in giving us his only Son unless we have experienced the love of a parent for a child and the devastating tragedy of a child predeceasing its parents?

Yet too often people judge their faith by childish standards. We mature in the love and appreciation of parents and family, but frequently fail to develop in our love of God and the faith. Some treat faith as a gift at baptism that never has to be developed. They go through life with the knowledge they gained in First Communion class. But that is like facing life with the knowledge of a first grader. As our knowledge of life expands, so our knowledge of God and the faith must grow. Faith is a love relationship with God. If we don't read, reflect, and pray, that relationship will wither and die. We have as much obligation to keep abreast of our faith as we do of current events. And we have as much obligation to nurture our relationship with God as we do with our parents, spouse, or children.

In the Emmaus episode Jesus reveals himself by explaining Scripture and by sharing a meal with the disciples in which he breaks bread. He does basically the same thing in his subsequent visit to the Apostles to bolster their faith. He first explains the meaning of the Scriptures, that the Messiah had to suffer and die, and then he shares a meal with them. Luke repeats the details to remind the Christian community that Jesus continues to do the same for us at each celebration of the Eucharist. First he offers us readings from Scripture that are subsequently explained and elucidated in a homily. Then he invites us to partake in the breaking of the bread which is his body given up for us. There is no better way to grow in the knowledge and love of God and to bolster our faith than participating in the Holy Sacrifice of the Mass. For there we are fed with deepening knowledge of Scripture and nourished with the Body and Blood of Jesus himself. Let us be grateful for God's gift to us of the Eucharist and Scripture and strive always to treasure them.

The Good Shepherd

The Shepherd image runs all through Scripture, from the first book to the last, from the Book of Genesis to the Book of Revelation. It is used to express God's unique relationship to Israel. In Genesis (48:15), as Jacob approaches death, he speaks lovingly of God "who has been my shepherd from my birth." In Revelation (7:17), John describes Jesus as the one who will shepherd the elect to "springs of life-giving water." We all know and love the 23rd Psalm: "My shepherd is the Lord." Isaiah speaks of God as a shepherd who gathers the lambs and leads the ewes (40:11). The shepherd image also carried over to God's special envoys. Jeremiah criticizes Israel's priests and kings, who were surrogates of Yahweh, as shepherds who mislead the flock (23:1). Ezekiel condemns them for pasturing themselves instead of the flock (34:2). Israel's two greatest leaders, also God's chosen deputies, were both originally shepherds. Moses was tending his father-in-law Jethro's flocks when God called him (Ex 3:1-2); David was summoned to be anointed while watching his father Jesse's sheep (1 S 16:11-13).

In the New Testament, as today's Gospel illustrates, Jesus freely applied the image to himself. Mark also uses shepherd imagery and metaphors for Jesus, as when he tells us Jesus pitied the crowds, who were like sheep without a shepherd (6:34). Jesus then proceeds to feed the people spiritually with his teaching and follows it up immediately by feeding them physically with the multiplication of the loaves and fish, a prefigurement of the Eucharist in which he will nourish us with food for eternal life. In using the shepherd metaphor Mark draws on Sirach who earlier referred to God in his compassion as "reproving, admonishing, teaching, as a shepherd guides his flock" (18:12). For humankind who had veered far from the ways of God, Jesus came to show the way, thus demonstrating he is truly the good shepherd. And since a good shepherd lays down his life for his sheep, submerged just below the surface of every reference to the good shepherd, is the notion of the passion and death of Jesus.

Till relatively late in Israel's history when they finally settled down to agriculture, the Jewish people were predominantly herdsmen tending their flocks. In choosing the metaphor of a shepherd for himself, God chose an image they knew well. We city folk, however, sometimes need help to recognize the earmarks of a good shepherd. A good shepherd had to be:

1. Nurturer and Provider. Palestine is in large part a barren, arid country. It offers little in terms of grass or flowing water. The shepherd had to provide pasture and water or the sheep would die.

2. Leader and Guide. With resources scarce, the shepherd had to scout out suitable sites for grazing and direct the sheep to them. Sheep are utterly incapable of foraging on their own. To appease their insatiable appetite for food, he had to keep the sheep moving. He had to know when and where to move them, always thinking a few days ahead. With scorching skies a good part of the year, the wise shepherd also planned his moves to keep the flock from the blazing sun, selecting a route on the shady side of the mountain or valley.

3. Preserver and Conserver. With the ecological system fragile in the Holy Land, the prudent shepherd also had to make sure the sheep did not overgraze an area and thereby destroy the delicate vegetation or trample upon a slowly gurgling spring and thus plug it up or redirect its trickling outflow underground.

4. Healer and Soother. Each night the shepherd had to check his sheep, bathing eyes irritated from sun and sand, pouring oil on thorn scratches, removing brambles from their fleece, taking pebbles from their hooves. In the intense heat, any untreated wound would soon fester, incapacitating and possibly killing the animal.

5. Defender and Protector. In ancient Palestine bears, wolves, and leopards roamed the countryside. If they had hungry cubs, kits, or pups at home, they would stop at nothing. Recall David honed

his skill with the slingshot that killed Goliath protecting his father's sheep from wild animals (1 S 17:34-36). Shepherds had to stand up to wild beasts and sometimes suffered the loss of life or limb.

6. Buffer and Shield. Jesus called himself the Sheep Gate. Searching for suitable pasture often took flock and shepherd far from home and the safety of a fenced corral. When forced to spend the night in the open fields, the shepherd had to search out a cave, gulch, or gully to enclose the flock. He would then lie down across the entrance to act as a buffer or gate. No sheep could wander off, no poacher enter, without stepping over him and waking him, thus forestalling rustlers, predators, and strays.

7. Knowledgeable about the Individual Sheep. Since flocks often had to share a cave or gully, shepherds had to be able to identify their sheep. One way they did this was to call them by name. Sheep, like dogs, respond to their name. To be a successful leader, the shepherd also had to know the idiosyncrasies and personalities of his sheep. Just as dogs and cats have distinct personalities, so do sheep. Two males, placed together, might fight; two yearlings might grow frisky. Young sheep tended to dart ahead; older ones often were sluggards and lagged behind. It took skill to keep them together, to have them function as a flock.

In sum, through the use of shepherd imagery God communicates to the world that his relationship with us is one of nurturer and provider, leader and guide, preserver and conserver, healer and soother, defender and protector, buffer and shield, one who knows us well, even to and despite our idiosyncrasies. Notice how similar in connotation the shepherd image is to God's other choice of title: Father or Parent. For parents are also nurturers and providers, leaders and guides, healers and soothers, defenders and protectors, ones who know us well, even to and despite our idiosyncrasies. Let us be ever thankful to God for his love for us and grateful to our parents, for all the love and care they have lavished upon us.

I Am the True Vine

We all know that an eagle is the symbol of the United States; a maple leaf, the symbol of Canada; a lion, the symbol of England; a hammer and sickle, the symbol of the former Soviet Union. But does anyone know off hand what the symbol of ancient Israel was? The symbol of ancient Israel was a grapevine. The Israelites etched it on their national coins and emblazoned it in pure gold above the entrance to the Temple over columns of solid white marble forty feet high, creating a dazzling vista for anyone entering the Temple on a typically sun-drenched day. How did a grapevine come to be the symbol for Israel?

A vineyard was a prized possession in the ancient Middle East. It provided a reliable beverage since water was generally not safe to drink. In an era before Valium, Xanax, Ativan, or Buspar it also provided a welcome source of relaxation. It offered an abundance of sweet, succulent fruit for hot summer days and, when dried as raisins, plenty of tasty winter morsels, for baking or snacking, at a desolate time of year when fresh fruits and vegetables were simply not available. Not surprisingly, therefore, ancient people lavished great care upon their vineyards, carefully planting the choicest vines, fencing them in with a stout wall for protection, and nurturing them assiduously over the generations. It is also not surprising that God chose the image of a vineyard to describe his special relationship with Israel, for over the years he had carefully selected them and cared for them, provided for them in their need and protected them in time of danger.

Vineyard imagery was often used in Scripture to describe both God's abiding love for Israel and his all too frequent disappointment in his people. In Jeremiah (2:21) God tells the Jewish people, "I had planted you, a choice vine of fully tested stock"; followed immediately by, "How could you turn out obnoxious to me, a spurious vine?" In the Song of the Vineyard, Isaiah speaks of God as a friend who had a vineyard in which he planted the choicest of vines expecting good grapes, only to get sour grapes. He then identifies Yahweh's vineyard as the House of Israel and the people of Judah as his cherished plant (Is 5:1-7). Psalm 80 (9-20) in turn speaks of Israel as a vine God uprooted from Egypt and planted in the Promised Land after having cleared out other nations to give it space to grow.

The Jewish people were well aware, then, of the vineyard imagery that was used of Israel in Scripture to convey both divine benediction and divine malediction. In applying the image of the true vine to himself, therefore, Jesus clearly suggests he supplants Israel. In Exodus (4:22-23) God referred to the Jewish people collectively as Israel for the first time and called them his son. In declaring he is the true vine, Jesus reveals he alone is the true son of God because, unlike Israel, he conforms his will to God's will perfectly in all things. Jesus then proceeds to develop some details from vine dressing that we have to understand to appreciate his meaning.

A fruitful vine requires considerable pruning. For the first three years it is not allowed to bear any fruit at all. Thereafter it is pruned severely each year at winter's end to stimulate spring growth. In summer it is trimmed again to remove offshoots and strengthen the branches most heavily ladened with blossoms. Even branches with relatively few blossoms are lopped off at this time to send a surge of strength to those more prolific. What is cut away is fit only for the home hearth. Wood of the vine is too soft for building and of no use for carpentry. It could not even be donated to the Temple as firewood for holocausts or sacrifices. Jesus thus presents a terribly stark contrast indeed between fruitful and non-fruitful branches!

Through the imagery of a vine, Jesus developed several important themes for his disciples. One is dependence. As a branch is useless and totally unproductive unless connected to the vine, so are we as Christians unless united to Jesus as the source and wellspring of our spiritual life and vitality. Viewed from a slightly different perspective, the vine image can also be understood in terms of unity. Unless the branches are united to the vine, they can produce nothing. Cut off from the vine, they inevitably wither and die. The vine image also speaks of sharing. It reminds us that through sanctifying grace we share in God's own divine life.

Lastly, Jesus used this vine imagery to teach his disciples and all who would come after them two important lessons. Jesus spoke these words at the Last Supper, just before he suffered and died. He had already warned his disciples that they too would have to suffer. There was no escape. The reference to pruning, then, may have been intended to strengthen their faith and give them some insight into the meaning and purpose of suffering. Through the pruning imagery Jesus suggests to the Apostles that the Father prunes the branches not as punishment but to render them more fruitful.

Jesus also uses the vine image to shed light on prayer. He assures his disciples that if they abide in him and his words stay part of them, the Father will answer their prayers. By this he means not that God will change his mind because of their closeness to Jesus and subsequently answer whatever they pray for, but that if they are truly close to Jesus and accept his teaching, they will adopt their ways to his, making what they pray for conform more closely to the Father's will and so more readily grantable.

Love One Another as I Have Loved You

John's Gospel is divided into two parts: the Book of Signs which deals with the three years of the public life of Jesus (chapters 1–12) and the Book of Glory which is devoted solely to the last week of Our Lord's life (chapters 13–21). The latter includes the passion and death of Jesus, when in John's theology the "hour" of Jesus had come. Today's Gospel comes from the Book of Glory. A major portion of this latter book in turn is given over to the words spoken by Jesus at the Last Supper, the night before he died. Spanning chapters 13 to 17 and representing Jesus' final legacy to his disciples, it is called the Final Discourse.

In style and structure Jesus' Final Discourse reflects a common literary form in Scripture. Great figures and leaders in the Old Testament typically delivered aloud the equivalent of their last will and testament before they died. Before he passed on, Jacob called his children together, blessed them, reminded them of all the good God had done for him and them, and asked God to keep them in his care (Gn 49). As Joshua approached his end, he summoned all of Israel before him, recalled all that God had enabled him and them to accomplish in driving the pagan nations from the land, asked them to be sure to fulfill the Mosaic Law, and above all to love Yahweh, their God (Jos 23-24). At the end of his life, before the whole assembly of Israel, David publicly proclaimed the glory of Yahweh and the mighty deeds performed on Israel's behalf. He then concluded with a prayer that his son Solomon would have the heart to keep God's commandments and at last build Yahweh a house or temple in Jerusalem (1 Ch 29:11-20). But the most famous farewell discourse of all was that of Moses, the great teacher, leader, and lawgiver of the Old Testament. It completely takes up the concluding chapters of Deuteronomy (29–34). In particular, Moses recalls a unique event in Jewish history, the giving of the

Ten Commandments, and asks his followers to remain true to God and the Decalogue.

The early Christians, most of whom were of Jewish descent, saw Jesus as the new Moses. This theme features most prominently in Matthew who wrote largely for his fellow Jewish converts. Here, however, John's presentation of Jesus' Final Discourse consciously calls to mind similarities with the farewell discourse of Moses. Just as Moses was the chief figure in the old dispensation who passed on God's Mt. Sinai revelation of the Ten Commandments, so Jesus is the chief figure in the new dispensation who gives us God's new command of perfect love. John thereby implies that this moment in time with the new commandment of self-sacrificing love is as important as God's revelation to Moses on Mt. Sinai. As the Ten Commandments were the basis for Israel's covenant relationship with Yahweh, so Jesus' new commandment of all-encompassing love is the foundation for a new covenant relationship with God.

Jesus' Farewell Discourse in John takes up four complete chapters (13-17). Today's Gospel with the command of perfect love is the central message. We know this because the Discourse begins and ends with a reference to love. It starts with "He loved his own in the world and he loved them to the end" (13:1), and ends with "...that the love with which you loved me may be in them, and I in them" (17:26). Today's passage is situated in the middle of the Discourse, which gives it prominence, and the command of perfect love is set in the middle of the passage. What Jesus has done is take all the commandments and boil them down to one. If we love one another as Jesus has loved us, we will indeed keep all the commandments.

Jesus then expounds on the type of love it should be. He is calling for a love that shows itself in action and sacrifice, even to the point of laying down one's life for a friend, as he will soon demonstrate on Calvary. Feelings and emotions are not enough; words, an inadequate substitute. At the time John wrote his Gospel, Gnostic tendencies were gnawing at the fiber of the early Christian community. The Gnostics believed sheer knowledge of God and awareness of self were sufficient for salvation. John in effect rejects this heretical belief by stressing Jesus' call for action, drastic action. He counters the beguiling deception that to know is to be saved with Jesus' unequivocal demand for deeds and self-sacrifice.

Jesus ends by calling those who follow his command his friends. Friends, from *philoi*, meaning "loved ones," are those we share our thoughts with. Slaves, by way of contrast, simply take orders and are not privy to the master's thoughts. To those who put his commands into practice, Jesus will reveal himself and his Father, thus showing them the way to everlasting life. This distinction in John between "slave" and "friend" is unique in the New Testament. Elsewhere, such as in Philemon (1:1) and Mark (10:44), for instance, the term "slave" or "servant" is used with positive overtones, connoting not one in the dark, but one totally dedicated to the service of the Lord.

It is also interesting that the term "friend" is never applied to God or Jesus directly, only to humankind. In the Old Testament we are told that God called Abraham his friend (Is 41:8) and talked with Moses face to face, as a man speaks with his friend (Ex. 33:11). In the New Testament Jesus speaks of his friend Lazarus sleeping (Jn 11:11). But "friend" was never a title used for the divinity. Friendship in the ancient Near East demanded reciprocity, with each party obligated to meet the legitimate expectations and demands of the other. God, by way of sharp and distinct contrast, is never obligated to anyone. Everything God does flows simply and solely from his gracious good will.

Jesus Ascends into Heaven

Jesus left the world the way he came into it: quietly, without fuss, in the presence of only a few who were especially dear to him. As we have often noted, the early Church was quick to see similarities between Jesus, the greatest figure in the New Testament, and Moses, the greatest figure in the Old Testament. Just as God revealed himself to Moses on a mountain (Mount Sinai), so Jesus revealed himself to his disciples in the Transfiguration on a mountain (Mount Tabor). Just as Moses first taught the law from a mountain (Mount Sinai), so Jesus first taught the fulfillment of the law in the Sermon on the Mount. Now we are reminded of similarities in their departures from this world.

In Deuteronomy, the last of the five books of the Torah, attributed to Moses himself, at the very end of the book, chapter 34, we read that Moses ascended Mount Nebo just before he died. There God showed him the Holy Land stretched out before him, the Promised Land that Moses would not be allowed to enter because he had doubted God at Meribah. Moses then dies on the mountain and is buried in the hills, but Deuteronomy concludes by adding that to this day no one knows where Moses is buried. This fueled speculation among pious Jews that Moses had been taken up into heaven like Elijah, his body too important to return to the earth. In today's Gospel, Mark is quick to point out that Jesus too was on a mountain when he was taken up into heaven, again similar to Moses and suggesting a reward for the very special life he led and the good he did.

Before departing, Jesus says to his disciples, "Go into the whole world and proclaim the gospel to every creature. Whoever believes and is baptized will be saved; whoever does not believe will be condemned." He is obviously speaking very seriously and with great authority. Up until the time of Jesus, such full power and authority had resided with Moses and the Mosaic Law he left behind. With the coming of Jesus, that power and authority passed to Jesus and was transformed and brought to completion. In Jesus the Law has been fulfilled and come to perfection. Moses' primitive ethic, an eye for an eye, a tooth for a tooth, introduced to curb the prevalent excesses of retribution and revenge, has been superseded by the far loftier and more demanding ethic: love your neighbor as yourself, and turn the other cheek. What Moses began, Jesus has brought to completion.

In his final command to baptize, Jesus makes three things clear. (1) Baptism now replaces circumcision as the introduction and sign of incorporation into God's family. (2) Jesus' disciples are not to be passive recipients but active spreaders of the Gospel message. We are all missioned by our Baptism to spread the good news. (3) Salvation is no longer restricted to the Jewish people but open to all nations and all people of every race, color, and nationality. God's mission for the Church is now truly universal.

What are we to learn from the Ascension? The Gospel today tells us that "after he spoke to them [Jesus] was taken up into heaven and took his seat at the right hand of the Father." To the modern mind this connotes separation: his task done, Jesus is now at home with his Father, far removed from the turmoil of the modern world. Yet the Gospel has the exact opposite intention. In ancient times, to sit at the right hand of someone meant the person had the other person's ear and therefore some influence with him. Sitting at the right hand of the king, for instance, was reserved for the queen, the highest ranking dignitary, or the specially invited guest—people who had access to and so could most easily sway the king. This notion of Jesus ascending to heaven and sitting at the right hand of the Father, then, was meant to convey that Jesus is now actively interceding for us with the Father, and that his role in the Church, far from having ceased, has rather intensified and switched in focus.

The message of the Ascension is, now that Jesus has returned to heaven, he is closer to us than ever. When Jesus was among us, he was limited by his physical body to a single place at a single time. With a human body circumscribed in time and space, he could not be everywhere. After his death and resurrection, however, he is no longer constrained by the limitations of a mortal body and continues to do good for the Church by interceding for us in heaven. In his stead, he sends the Holy Spirit, the third person of the Blessed Trinity, to be with us. Thus, the triune God maintains an active presence and participation in today's world and Church through the Holy Spirit, while God the Son remains at the Father's right hand interceding for us. In short, far from speaking of God's withdrawal or retreat from the world, the Ascension actually signals more intensive involvement on two fronts, with Jesus interceding for us in heaven and the Holy Spirit actively engaged in the work of the Church on earth.

Mark began his Gospel with reference to Jesus Christ as the Son of God: God is with us. He ends his Gospel with Jesus' working with the disciples, confirming their preaching through accompanying signs. Thus, Mark begins and ends his Gospel with the notion of God always with us in the person of Jesus Christ. A beautiful thought for Ascension Day.

The Great High Priestly Prayer

Today's Gospel is from John. I would like to say something about the Gospel of John in general and then something about today's passage in particular. John's Gospel is different from all the others. As the last evangelist to set his Gospel down in writing, John could assume his audience was familiar with the basic details of the life of Jesus from the previously published accounts of his predecessors. This gave him the luxury of developing his Gospel more as a theological reflection and overview of Jesus' life and mission, rather than simply as a historical or biographical narrative. The end result is a tightly structured, highly stylized Gospel. John carefully chose and selected his material, arranged it and positioned it, to provide richer insights and bring to the surface otherwise hidden connections.

John's Gospel is divided into two parts: the Book of Signs (chs. 1-12) and the Book of Glory (chs. 13-21). The Book of Signs covers the whole public life of Jesus up to but excluding the last week of his life, a time span of some three years. The Book of Glory, on the other hand, is devoted solely to the final week of Jesus' life on earth, reflecting the overwhelming importance theologically to John and the early Church of Jesus' passion and death. Though covering a considerably broader base and longer time span, the Book of Signs offers a surprisingly stringent selection of events from the life of Jesus, with each carefully chosen for theological relevance and insight. Of the many miracles and wondrous works Jesus wrought, John mentions only seven. John typically refers to the miracles as signs because they reveal God's presence or glory at work in Jesus. Each sign in turn is invariably followed by a discourse or discussion by Jesus to show how the miracle fits into his overall mission or illustrates some facet of his ultimate goal.

I'll cite two brief illustrations. John mentions the multiplication of the loaves (6:1-15) as one of the seven signs/miracles. Shortly thereafter, he records Jesus' discourse on the living bread (6:35-40). The miracle, then, is clearly intended to bolster the faith of the audience for the subsequent revelation of the Eucharist. In the cure of the man born blind (9:1-41), another of the seven signs, the man not only gains physical sight but eventually knowledge and faith in Jesus as well. John then follows the cure with the discourse of the Good Shepherd in which Jesus declares, "I know mine and mine know me" (10:14). John's purpose in juxtaposing the two is precisely to show Jesus came to remove the blindness that keeps us from him and lead us to knowledge and faith in him.

In the second half of his Gospel, the Book of Glory, the power and glory of God at work in Jesus that began to manifest itself in the miracles Jesus performed earlier come to full flowering. To make it even more powerful and dramatic, John deliberately reverses the order of his presentation. Instead of explaining a deed by a subsequent discourse, John begins the Book of Glory with a discourse to explain the single deed that is to follow, i.e., the passion and death of Jesus. Thus, the first half of the Book of Glory is devoted solely to the words Jesus spoke at the Last Supper (chs. 13-17), which in turn is called the Final Discourse. What we read from today, the end of the Final Discourse, is known as the High Priestly Prayer, for Jesus ended his words to his disciples at the Last Supper with a prayer. For all practical purposes, this prayer represents the last words Jesus spoke before he died, the last thoughts he wished to communicate to us. For upon leaving the Last Supper Jesus hardly spoke again, neither when questioned by Pontius Pilate who had the power to release him, nor when suffering through the excruciating pain of the crucifixion and its preliminaries. From this point on in the Gospel, John ignores the spoken word and concentrates all his attention on the deed, what Jesus did to redeem and save us.

The High Priestly Prayer (ch. 17) falls into three parts. First Jesus prays for himself (v. 1-8), then he prays for his disciples (v. 9-19), and finally he prays for all those who will one day believe in him (v. 20-26), which includes all of us present here today. Today's Gospel reading comes from the middle section in which Jesus prays for his disciples. He prays that God will protect them, just as he has guarded them and kept watch over them, using the shepherd imagery he had used earlier in the Good Shepherd discourse. He speaks of his disciples as a gift from God, referring to them as those "you have given me" (17:11). He declares they are precious to him because they share his life, just as he shares his Father's life, and he asks God to keep them in his name. By this he asks God to continue the intimate bond between him and them that they might remain in the intimate love of his Father which they share through him.

John then resorts to his familiar use of the word, "world," to connote those who oppose God's views and prefer the way of the world. Since his disciples have demonstrated they are not of this mindset, people who are materially-minded will oppose them. Jesus asks not that they be taken out of this ungodly atmosphere, but that they simply not be tainted by it or succumb to it. Rather, they are to be a catalyst to bring about change, a leaven to help good will spread and proper judgment take root. At the conclusion of today's reading we see Jesus ask that his disciples be sent just as he was sent. As he consecrated himself and made himself holy, so he wishes his disciples to be holy and dedicated to God's will so that they can spread God's message and bring all people to his love. With his death imminent and the ascension not far off, if the Church was to continue, he knew full well it would have to be through the effort of his disciples. Let us pray that we rise to the challenge.

The Acts of the Apostles

The following is provided as an alternate to a traditional Pentecost homily on the basic details of the feast, such as is offered for Pentecost in Cycle A. It may also provide some background for the Easter season readings.

The first reading for Pentecost in all three liturgical cycles comes from Luke's Acts of the Apostles. The Acts of the Apostles chronicles the history of the primitive Church as the Holy Spirit worked within the original disciples of Jesus first to solidify their individual faith and then to forge them into a community of believers that would gradually increase in number and eventually carry the Good News to the four corners of the earth. Since selections from Acts completely dominate the readings of the seven weeks of the post-Easter liturgical season, it is helpful to understand the overall sweep and structure of this masterful history of the early Church by Luke. The best secondary source I have found is Raymond E. Brown, *A Once-and-Coming Spirit at Pentecost* (Collegeville: Liturgical Press, 1994). The following borrows from Brown and is at best a brief and inadequate recap of the aforementioned book.

Luke's Acts takes up where Luke's Gospel left off, namely at the ascension of Jesus. The Apostles return to Jerusalem and their first act of business is to elect a successor to Judas, the one who betrayed Jesus. They winnow out two candidates who have been with them from the beginning and have witnessed all that Jesus said and did during his public life. Then, after prayer, they select Matthias by lot (1:15-26). But from the Gospel accounts we know they were still fearful and hesitated to leave their locked quarters, let alone preach the Good News. Then on the Jewish feast of Pentecost the Holy Spirit descended upon them and changed their lives forever. The Spirit filled them with courage, wisdom, and zeal, plus the unique ability to communicate with people of different languages. Peter begins to preach at once and immediately 3000 people are added to their number (2:1-41). The Jewish religious authorities grow alarmed by their teaching of the resurrection of Jesus and order them to stop. The Sadducees, the priestly members of the Sanhedrin, spearheaded this initial opposition in part because their publicly proclaimed religious beliefs precluded any hope of resurrection or an afterlife. But the Apostles are enflamed by the Spirit and there can be no turning back. They continue to preach fearlessly and another 5000 are added to their ranks. The high priest has the Apostles arrested but they are miraculously freed by an angel during the night. The first section of Acts then ends with the Christian community united in heart and soul (4:1-5:42).

By chapter 6 the first signs of strain begin to appear in the Jerusalem Church between those of Hebrew and Hellenistic descent. The Hebrews were those who were born as Jews and though accepting Jesus still felt compelled to follow the Mosaic Law and worship in the Temple. The Hellenists were Greek converts to Judaism who saw no need for Jewish law or Temple services once they had accepted Jesus. To pressure the Hellenist faction into conformity, the more numerous Hebrew members scaled back the community's charitable dole to widows of Greek descent. Called in as mediators, the Apostles sided with fairness and created a new office of deacons to oversee the distribution of food and alms (6:1-7).

The Hellenists' attitude toward the Temple, however, rekindled official Jewish opposition that led to bitter persecution of this subsector of Christianity. Stephen was an ardent Hellenist who preached to foreign Jews. Misconstruing Stephen's teaching about Jesus destroying the temple, they accuse him of threatening their sacred Temple. He is hauled before the Sanhedrin where he pleads his case and expounds the Christian doctrine most eloquently, but the outcome is rigged against him from the start. He is dragged outside the city walls and stoned to death, the first to shed his blood for the faith (7:1-60). This signals the start of the first major persecution of the Church. Though confined to the Hellenist Christians who opposed Temple worship, it sent many scurrying for safety and occasioned the start of a major missionary movement. As the refugees fled they brought the Gospel message with them and bore witness to it through their suffering. Philip had great success in Samaria among kindred spirits who also keenly opposed the Jerusalem Temple (8:4-8). He also enjoyed unique success with an Ethiopian eunuch struggling to interpret the prophet Isaiah. Though the eunuch's altered state would automatically preclude entrance into Judaism (Dt 23:2), Philip has no qualm or hesitation baptizing him into Christianity (8:26-40), an early sign of the Church's openness to all.

The conversion of Saul, the apostle to the Gentiles, takes up the bulk of the next two chapters. In the interim the persecution of the Hellenist Christians intensified, sending them farther afield in search of safe havens. Wherever they went, they preached the Good News. Fresh from his conversion, Paul joins their missionary effort in Antioch at Barnabas' invitation (11:26). They start in the synagogues but soon move on to the Gentiles where the response is greater. As they work among the Gentiles, the relevance of Jewish dietary laws and the need for circumcision are challenged and questioned. Though once a strict Pharisee, Paul eventually convinces Peter and the Jerusalem Church that neither dietary observance nor circumcision is required to be a true follower of Jesus. This decision proves fateful and sets the whole Christian community at odds with the Jewish authorities. The Pharisees join the Sadducees in opposition to the Christians and Jewish persecution spreads to Hebrew as well as Hellenist members of the Church.

In deference to his primacy, Acts portrays Peter as the first to make exceptions for the Gentiles. With dietary laws considered an essential part of revelation, a heavenly vision and voice are required to prompt and support Peter's decision to dispense from these regulations (10:1-16; 11:1-18). Peter is also portrayed as the first to officially waive the requirement of circumcision into the Jewish religion before being baptized a Christian when he orders Cornelius and his household, all Gentiles, to be baptized immediately in the name of Jesus (10:44-48).

While Acts is commonly regarded as a history of the early Church, on this feast of Pentecost we can also see it as an account of the Holy Spirit at work in the first believers. From this vantage point we see the Holy Spirit at first strengthening the faith of the early disciples—their faith in Jesus and their faith in themselves. With both bolstered, they throw open the locked doors they have been cowering behind and go forth to preach the Good News as Jesus taught them. The Holy Spirit inspires their words, as Jesus promised he would, and they make many converts among the Jews in Jerusalem. When persecution breaks out, they fan out from Jerusalem and make still more converts. As they move farther away from the Jewish world, they come into increasing contact with Gentiles. Under the Spirit's guidance, many of the Gentiles are drawn to accept Jesus and the Church learns to accommodate them by distinguishing between what is truly essential and what is not in Old Testament law and tradition. In a relatively short time the Church reaches Rome, the center of the civilized world at the time, and though suffering violent persecutions there, eventually becomes the official religion of the Roman Empire.

God Speaks from Mountains High

A homily specifically tailored for the theme of Trinity Sunday is offered under Trinity Sunday in Cycle A. Here we work simply with the Gospel assigned for today which, though beautiful in its message and important for its overall relevance to Matthew's Gospel, is rather better suited to the Feast of the Ascension.

Today's Gospel reading comes from the final scene of Matthew's Gospel. Here we see Jesus ascend into heaven from a mountaintop. In the mountain setting we can find a reprise of all of Matthew's Gospel. Steeped as he was in Jewish customs and Old Testament tradition, Matthew typically used a mountain setting as the site of important revelations. Just as the Old Testament reports that God revealed himself to Moses and Elijah on Mt. Sinai, also known as Mt. Horeb, so Matthew records that Jesus revealed important information about himself and his mission on mountain or elevated locations. If we look closely at today's reading, we will find the different themes of these previous revelations are all masterfully caught up and subsumed in Matthew's conclusion.

The first mountain backdrop for a revelation in Matthew's Gospel appears in the Temptation of Jesus by Satan in the desert. In the third and final temptation Satan takes Jesus to a high mountain to show him all the kingdoms of the world. He then promises to give Jesus all these kingdoms if he will worship him. But Jesus drives the devil away with the words from Deuteronomy (6:13): "The Lord, your God, shall you fear (worship); him shall you serve." For being true to his Father, God will eventually give Jesus dominion over all the world. As Jesus tells the disciples in today's Gospel, "All power in heaven and on earth has been given to me."

Matthew is also careful to record that Jesus chose an elevated spot to begin his public teaching (Mt 5:1). That teaching has come down to us in what is popularly known as the Sermon on the Mount.

103

It is worth noting that although Jesus commissioned his disciples to proclaim the kingdom of God and to cure the sick (Mt 10:5-8), he never enjoined them to teach. In fact he told them they should not even consider themselves teachers for there was only one teacher, the Christ (Mt 23:10). He deliberately restrained his disciples from teaching others until his final departure, when his mission was completed and they finally understood the full Gospel message, namely that Jesus had to suffer, die, and be raised from the dead in accord with the Father's will. Now with their education complete and him ready to return to his Father, Jesus formally gives them the mandate to teach. On the mountaintop to which he has summoned them, at the very end of Matthew's Gospel, he charges them, "Go, therefore, and make disciples of all the nations, baptizing them in the name of the Father, and of the Son, and of the Holy Spirit, teaching them to observe all that I have commanded you."

It was likewise on a mountain that the Transfiguration took place (Mt 17:1-8). In this critically important revelation the Apostles were strengthened for the upcoming ordeal of the passion and death of Jesus. In a vision with Moses and Elijah, symbolic representatives of the Law and Prophets, the major source of revelation up to that point in time, Jesus is transformed before Peter, James, and John. God's voice from a cloud, an Old Testament symbol for God, is heard to say, "This is my beloved Son with whom I am well pleased." At the end of the vision Moses and Elijah disappear and Jesus is left standing alone, indicating that from that moment on he is to be the sole source of revelation. Confirming this fact before finally ascending into heaven, Jesus declares, "All power in heaven and on earth has been given to me."

An elevated location also marked the site of the Agony in the Garden. While Matthew identifies the specific site as Gethsemane (Mt 26:36), Luke describes the general area as the Mount of Olives (Lk 22:39). Here Jesus underwent such profound mental suffering and anguish in anticipation of what awaited him in his imminent passion and death that in Luke's description of the event we are told blood mingled with Jesus' sweat (Lk 22:44). In today's Gospel, set on a similar mountain or mount, Jesus tells his disciples to go out to all the nations and teach them all they have been privileged to witness, most importantly his passion and death which began in the Agony in the Garden on the Mount of Olives.

The climactic moment of the life of Jesus, his crucifixion and death on the cross, also took place on elevated ground, on a mound shaped like a skull, called "Golgotha" in Aramaic and "Calvary" in Latin (Mt 27:33). On Calvary Jesus demonstrated such perfect submission to God's will in laying down his life without a cry or complaint that the Roman centurion in charge of his execution felt compelled to exclaim, "Truly this was the Son of God" (Mt 27:54). In today's Gospel, when Jesus declares all power has been given him, the Apostles realize that Jesus and the Father are one. They too come to realize that Jesus is truly the Son of God.

The mountain location as the site of the Ascension of Jesus at the end of Matthew's Gospel thus helps to stir up memories of important events in the public life of Jesus, all of which share a common thread of having happened on a mountain or elevation. Matthew also designed the end of his Gospel to round out and enrich a theme he introduced at the very beginning of his Gospel. There he presented the birth of Jesus as the fulfillment of Isaiah (7:14): "The virgin will be with child, and bear a son, and shall name him Immanuel," a name which Matthew (1:23) tells us means "God is with us." Now at the end of his Gospel, in the very last line of text, Matthew reminds us that Jesus did indeed fulfill this prophecy of Isaiah with his final assurance to the disciples and Church: "And behold, I am with you always, until the end of the age."

St. Charles Lwanga and his Companions

Charles Lwanga is one of my favorite saints and a truly remarkable man by any norm or standard. He and his fourteen companions were martyred during a persecution of Christianity in Uganda in the late nineteenth century. Their king, Mwanga, at first allowed Christian missionaries to enter the land as part of an overall treaty with European powers that he hoped would enrich him and the royal treasury with increased opportunities for trade and commerce. The king himself seemed to warm to Christianity in the beginning but this might have been simply part of a show to curry favor with the foreign elite. When the missionaries grew critical of his behavior, however, particularly his insatiable lust for power, possessions, and pleasure, he quickly banished them from the land. By this time a number of his people had converted to Christianity, and still more were in training as catechumens. Suddenly they found themselves cut off from all spiritual guidance and deprived of the sacraments, most notably the Holy Eucharist. Neophytes in the faith, they were left totally on their own to cope with an increasingly menacing environment as their paranoid and megalomaniacal king edged closer and closer to the brink of depravity and madness.

At the time of the expulsion of the missionaries Charles Lwanga was in charge of the pages at court. Pages were drawn from the best and the brightest young men in the land, usually from the most influential families. The position was basically an internship at court, a chance to meet all the important people in power and learn the ways of the government. It was a stepping-stone to a promising career that most parents craved for their children. Among the pages were fourteen Christians, though many of them were still catechumens. Charles baptized four of the catechumens he thought ready and tried his best to shield them all from the pagan atmosphere at court.

Once rid of the missionaries' presence, Mwanga plunged deeper and deeper into promiscuity. His banquets frequently turned to orgies. Charles was careful to assign the Christian pages elsewhere on such occasions but some mischief-maker eventually betrayed him to the king. Enraged, Mwanga ordered the Christian pages to attend the next banquet. When they refused, explaining their new religion would not permit them to do so, he took it as a personal insult and ordered them imprisoned. Their families pleaded for them with the king and he responded with an ultimatum. The young men would either attend the next banquet or face public execution. The families then begged their sons to accede to the king's wishes, but to the man and boy (one was only 13), they refused even though, as pages, they had witnessed the king's savagery in executing those who defied him.

The penalty for defying the king, they well knew, was to be burned alive. They would each be tied in the middle of a bundle of reeds and faggots and knocked over so they would end up lying flat on the ground. The fire would then be lit at their feet so that it would consume them slowly and painfully before coming to any vital organ that might kill them quickly. They would also be compelled to carry the reeds and faggots that would incinerate them the several circuitous miles to the execution site. The journey was designed not only to make them a public spectacle throughout the region but also to give them time to think of what lay ahead and afford their families and friends a final chance to dissuade them. But they all remained firm in their conviction and resigned to their fate. Charles Lwanga was singled out by the head executioner for exceptionally cruel treatment in part for his leadership role but also in part to settle up old scores of a bitter rivalry in which Charles had consistently overshadowed him in advancing at court. Charles never complained of his butchery and to the very end was heard praying for forgiveness for his persecutors.

What I find so remarkable about St. Charles Lwanga and his companions is the circumstances in which they died. None of them had a personal history or tradition of Christianity on which to draw. They say it takes three generations before the faith is firmly founded in a new land. But these young men from Uganda willingly died for the faith within a very few years of hearing the Gospel. It is never easy to lay down one's life but I think it would be easier to die for a major tenet of the faith such as the existence of God or the divinity of Jesus than for a moral principal or virtue such as chastity. To lay down one's life rather than commit an act that everyone else in the country, from king on down, was doing and enjoying is nothing less than extraordinary. While most of us depend on the influence of families and friends to help us stay on the straight and narrow, these young men had to stand up against strong opposing family pressure. We all hope to have access to a priest and the sacraments before we die. These great martyrs for the faith did not even have that final help or consolation. They didn't have a priest to help them form their conscience in the most difficult and important decision of their lives. They didn't have a priest to hear their last confession, nor did they have the comfort of Holy Viaticum, one's last Communion in which Jesus comes to escort the dying person on the final journey home.

On this wonderful feast of Corpus Christi when we celebrate God's inestimable gift to us in the Eucharist, let us pray that we always be grateful and strive to receive the Eucharist frequently and with devotion, mindful that many people, including the martyrs of Uganda, have not been blessed with the easy access we enjoy. Let us also thank God that we have never experienced in our country a ruler or persecution that has deprived us of the Eucharist or the opportunity to practice our faith openly and freely.

Let us also pray for the people of Uganda and all of Africa, many of whom live in turmoil today. And let the sterling example of these brave martyrs of Uganda dispel any chauvinistic attitudes we might have about the so-called Dark Continent. With so many dismal and depressing reports coming out of Africa these days, we sometimes wonder if anything good can come out of that troubled continent. When we think this way, let us ask ourselves how many young men we could find in the United States today who would be willing to lay down their lives simply to avoid a lascivious party hosted at a palace by the ruler of the land? How many people, young or old, of either sex, would face death by fire rather than violate a single moral principle? How many more would likely vie for admission to such an event and spend substantial time and money to pore over the tabloid coverage and gape at the videotaped recordings? Yet over a hundred years ago in darkest Africa, when Christianity was just dawning, fourteen young men freely and courageously laid down their lives under the cruelest of circumstances rather than offend God in the least.

Plucking Grain, Healing the Man
with the Withered Hand

Today's Gospel deals with the last two conflicts in a series of five which Mark presents between various religious authorities and Jesus at the beginning of his Gospel. Both provoked by the Pharisees, these two concluding conflicts ostensibly center on what the Pharisees perceive as violations of the Sabbath rest, but in fact are little more than thinly veiled challenges to Jesus' authority. The first charge stems from the Apostles' picking grain on the Sabbath; the second, from Jesus' curing a man with a withered hand also on the Sabbath.

The first controversy results from the Pharisees' spying on Jesus. As Jesus and his disciples walk along, the Pharisees detect the disciples plucking heads of grain from the fields. Mosaic Law permitted whatever one could take by hand as long as no sickle was used (Dt 23:26). But this was the Sabbath and Mosaic Law forbade work on the Sabbath (Ex 34:21). It is debatable whether plucking a few heads of grain constituted work as proscribed in the Torah, but Pharisaic ingenuity had divined and devised more than three dozen subcategories of servile work that included reaping, gleaning, winnowing, and threshing. Jesus knew better than to reason with the absurd Pharisaic logic and so falls back on an old rabbinical technique. He defends the Apostles' conduct with a parallel from Scripture.

Jesus refers to the unusual experience of David who, when fleeing with his men from Saul, went to the sanctuary at Nob and asked for bread to sate their hunger (1 S 21). The priest Ahimelech, whom Mark incorrectly identifies as Abiathar, had nothing but sacred bread, called showbread. Leviticus (24:5-9) prescribed that twelve loaves of finest wheat were to be placed on a golden table before Yahweh each week, carefully laid out in two rows of six as a memorial offering in perpetuity. When replaced each week, the bread was sacred and to be consumed only by the priests. David nevertheless ate the consecrated bread and shared it with his men. Jesus cites the incident as scriptural proof that human need takes precedent over ritual law, even divinely inspired ritual law.

Jesus then concludes this particular controversy with a proverb resonating with the spirit of Genesis (2:1-3), to wit, the Sabbath is made for man, not man for the Sabbath. In a subsistence economy people have to work to eat. But they can also work themselves to death for material gain and kill any chance of a meaningful relationship with God, family, or friends. The first reading from Deuteronomy addresses this danger. Here God directs his people to reserve one day each week for him and each other. It is to be a day when all will be free to rest and profit from each other's company: God, there as always for humankind, and humankind with the time and leisure to respond without distraction to God and loved ones in the simple joy of being together. Sabbath rest in God's plan was designed to liberate all creatures, Jesus thus suggests, not to limit their freedom or curb life's pleasures. But Sabbath rest as it evolved under the scribes and Pharisees, history shows, proved so restrictive and oppressive that people ended up prisoners of the day, not its beneficiaries.

The second confrontation in today's Gospel and the final one in the series of five is the most pernicious. It is both provoked and premeditated on the part of the Pharisees who anticipated correctly Jesus would cure the man with the withered hand despite the Sabbath. Curing on the Sabbath also fell under the purview of servile work and the distinctions drawn were draconian. Medical attention was permitted only in dire emergencies or life-threatening situations. Within these stringent parameters treatment was further circumscribed to merely preventing death or deterioration of the person's condition. Nothing could be done to speed recovery or alleviate the pain. One could staunch a wound, but not set a bone; bandage a cut, but apply no oil.

The extremes to which orthodox Jews felt bound by Sabbath

rest restrictions is best illustrated and documented in terms of military history. In war after war, devout Jews refused to pick up their swords on the Sabbath even to defend their own lives. The Romans who were notorious for conscripting conquered people as cannon fodder for their legions barred all Jews from military service for precisely this reason. They were a danger to themselves and their units. When besieging Jerusalem in 63 BC, Pompey diabolically took advantage of the population's blind adherence to the Sabbath. By working solely on the Sabbath, he was able to build a ramp against the outer wall of the city unimpeded. The Jews within knew he would use the ramp to breach the wall and take the city, but they never lifted a finger to stop him because all the work was confined to the Sabbath when they could lift neither stone nor sword to thwart him.

Knowing the Pharisees' enmity towards him and their rigid adherence to the minutiae of the law, Jesus at first tries to liberate them and their thinking with a simple question, "Is it lawful to do good on the Sabbath rather than evil, to save life rather than destroy it?" Law is made for the good of humankind and falls into two categories, moral law and social law. Moral law is designed to help us live ethically, according to our nature. Social law, which includes ritual law, is intended to help us get along with each other. Moral law admits of no exceptions. Social laws are subject to hierarchies and changing circumstances. While it is always right to do good and avoid evil, time and circumstances sometimes determine what is right and wrong. In the Parable of the Good Samaritan, for example, a priest and Levite are the first to spy the injured man. But they are more concerned with avoiding ritual impurity, which in itself is good, than neglecting a person in need, which is bad. They would have done better to forget about ritual impurity and tend to the man. By analogy, Jesus indicates here it is better to set aside the ritual law of Sabbath observance for the moral law of aiding one in need. Consequently, Jesus has no qualms about curing the man on the Sabbath. He knew anyone with an open mind would see the justification of the cure.

Jesus' Family and Beelzebul

Today's Gospel is full of shocks and surprises. Three charges are leveled against Jesus: he is out of his mind, he is possessed by Beelzebul, and he is an agent of Satan. The first accusation is brought by members of Jesus' extended family, the second and third by a delegation of scribes from Jerusalem. The first shock is his family claims he has taken leave of his senses. They may have completely misunderstood him and his mission, concluding he had overextended himself physically (no time to eat, no place to lay his head) or intellectually (a carpenter's son from Nazareth daring to stand up to the religious authorities from Jerusalem). But they may also have been more clever and well intentioned than first appears.

By now Jesus had provoked some powerful religious authorities with his teaching and miracles and everyone knew this could bring dire consequences. The Pharisees and Herodians were in fact already plotting to kill him (Mk 3:6). His relatives had good reason, therefore, to fear for both his safety and, by extension, the family's good name. They may simply have been trying to help him and save their own reputations and standings in the community. A plea of temporary mental instability would help excuse his conduct and exonerate them from guilt by association. But Jesus would have none of it. Even with the best intentions, his family was out of sync with his calling, at odds with his ministry.

The second shock is the depths to which the scribes were willing to stoop to discredit Jesus. They claim he is possessed by Beelzebul and cures only with Satan's help. The charge is vapid, clearly contradicted by the facts. Sickness was regarded as the result of sin leading to a loss of well-being and varying degrees of control by evil spirits. In curing people beset with various diseases including outright possession by demons, Jesus has been publicly beating back the forces of evil to the astonishment of all. For one

113

allegedly in cahoots with the devil, this is strange conduct indeed. His cures counter Satan's hold on humankind, not strengthen it. Why, Jesus asks, would someone aligned with Satan work against him? Why would Satan ever consider helping someone to destroy his very power base? To the contrary, Jesus' cures demonstrate he is more powerful than Satan, capable of subduing him, and is in the midst of despoiling him of his property.

Jesus came to forgive sin. His mention of a sin that cannot be forgiven, therefore, also comes as a shock. The unforgivable sin is to attribute the power to forgive sin, not to God who alone can forgive sin, but to evil forces who have no power or will to do so. Anyone looking to the evil one to forgive sin, has no hope of being forgiven. Worse, such a one blasphemes by denying God his legitimate power or due. To attribute the works of Jesus to Satan and not to God is the unforgivable sin precisely because the perpetrator deliberately and purposefully cuts himself off from and repudiates the source of forgiveness.

The next shock comes from Mark's report of Jesus' mother and "brothers" waiting outside. Catholic tradition has long held that Jesus was the only child of Mary. The confusion arises because Hebrew had no word for "cousin." Relatives of the same generation, such as cousins of any degree, were simply called brothers or sisters. St. Jerome, father of ancient biblical scholarship, took "brothers" to mean "cousins" in this context. The Greek word used to translate "brother" also does not require having the same set of parents. Wide extensions of the concept of brother/sister are also common in many languages, including English. Fraternities induct new brothers each year, sororities welcome new sisters. At Mass each day the priest says, "Pray, my brothers and sisters." Yet none speaks of biological connection. Some modern Scripture scholars would like to speculate otherwise but they have long-standing tradition to contend with. Mary's perpetual virginity was unquestionably held by Athanasius who fondly used the term "ever-virgin." It was also commonly accepted by the Fathers of both the East and West from the fifth century onwards.

The fifth shock stems from Jesus' seeming disclaimer of his mother and extended family. "Who are my mother and my brothers?" In ancient times family came first and blood was decidedly thicker than water. Family members had first claim on one's time, talent, and treasure. People would naturally expect Jesus to make way for his family at once. But Mark deliberately portrays them "outside" physically, while those who listen to Jesus are "inside" with him. The point, as Jesus explains with the words, "Whoever does the will of God is my brother and sister and mother," is that in the kingdom of God one's rank and proximity to Jesus is not based on bonds of blood or biology but solely by devotion and obedience to God's will. It marks a complete reversal of this world's standards and practices and in no way demeans Mary. As one who perfectly fulfilled God's will in all things from the first moment of her conception, Mary is the one closest of all to Jesus in faith and practice as well as in blood.

The final and biggest shock to his immediate audience was that blood didn't count, loyalty did; family no longer mattered, service was key. Mark reinforces this revolutionary notion by deliberately dividing the reaction of Jesus' family into two parts and then sandwiching between them, like two pieces of bread, the controversy with the scribes over his healing and exorcisms. He does so to emphasize that Jesus will continue to heal and liberate, thus vanquishing the forces of evil in the world, not through his biological family but through a group of faithful followers who will emulate his example and put into practice his law of perfect love.

Parables of a Germinating Seed
and the Mustard Seed

Today's Gospel is from the fourth chapter of Mark. At the very beginning of Mark's Gospel, Jesus announces the reign of God is at hand. Then Mark tells us Jesus taught in the synagogues with authority and the people were astonished by his teaching. But Mark never tells us what it was that Jesus taught. For the first three chapters he only tells us what Jesus did, the cures he worked and the conflicts he had with the Jewish religious authorities. It's only in chapter four that Mark finally begins to lay out the teaching of Jesus and he begins the exposition with a series of parables all joined by the common theme of seed.

To understand the teaching and parables we should see them in context. Shortly before the parables, Jesus calls his Apostles (Mk 3:13-19). He invites them to follow him, to be with him. They accept and will remain close to him through the rest of the Gospel. But then Jesus meets with rejection (Mk 3:20-22). The scribes refuse to put faith in him, claiming Satan is the source of his miraculous powers. They harden their hearts against Jesus and are soon joined by other religious and secular leaders such as the Pharisees and Herodians. Next Mark records a strange incident that sheds light on the previous two (Mk 3:31-35). Mary and the relatives of Jesus come in search of him and when Jesus is told they are outside, he replies enigmatically that his mother and brothers are those who do God's will. It seems harsh at first but when we recall Mary fulfilled the will of God perfectly at every moment of her life, always putting into practice the glorious Fiat she expressed to the Father at the Annunciation, we realize Mary was close to Jesus not merely through blood but more so through her faith-filled response to God's every wish. By analogy, the point Jesus makes to his Jewish audience is that even though they are descendants of Abraham by birth, that biological connection alone is not enough to make them God's people. They must also have faith and do the work of God, as their father Abraham did before them.

With this as the immediate background and backdrop, Mark begins to set forth the teaching of Jesus in parables. The first, not read today, tells of a sower sowing seed (Mk 4:3-9). Some fell on good ground and yielded a hundredfold harvest. Some fell on poor soil where it withered and died. The seed is the word of God. From the context of what preceded it, the good soil is suggestive of the Apostles who were open to God's will and hence will be fruitful in spreading the word of God. The poor soil, on the other hand, suggests the scribes who smothered God's word before it could ever take root in their hearts. Mark subsequently tells us that Jesus continued to develop his teaching with the Apostles because they were receptive, but not with the scribes who had closed their minds against him. This supports the point of the parable of the lamp which comes immediately before the parables we read today: "To the one who has, more will be given; from the who has not, even what he has will be taken away" (Mk 4.24).

The two parables we read today continue in this vein. The first is a little unusual and appears only in Mark. In it Jesus simply describes how a seed grows, selecting wheat as his example. First a thin blade or sprout appears, turns into a stalk with a tiny ear, and then the ear fills with grain until it is ripe for harvest. The point of the parable is that the kingdom of God, which is more accurately translated the reign of God, is like the seed. If we open our hearts to the word of God and allow the Spirit of God to work within us, without our knowing how, our faith will deepen and the kingdom of God will spread. Mother Teresa, as all the great saints, was acutely aware of God working through her. When challenged that she and her ministry could never meet all the needs of India's poor, she replied, "I am not called to be successful, I am called to be faithful." She well understood her own insignificance and the centrality of God's saving grace.

The second parable also tells of a seed but talks in terms of a contrast in size. From small beginnings, great things come: from a tiny seed, a towering elm; from a small acorn, a mighty oak. Here Jesus chooses an example germane to Palestine, a mustard seed. The tiniest of seeds, it grows into a shrub that reaches ten feet in height and produces a valuable crop. Its seeds are prized for oil and as a tangy spice. The point of the parable is that from the humblest beginnings the kingdom of God can also grow. Scripture is filled with references to the mighty cedars of Lebanon, a tall, majestic tree that grew on lofty mountaintops. In choosing the image of a mustard shrub which grew like a weed in the fields and in empty lots, Jesus also implies the kingdom of God is growing all around us, even in our own backyards.

What did these parables mean to the early Church and what do they tell us today? The first parable was addressed to the Apostles and early disciples who wondered how they, unlettered and inarticulate, could ever hope to spread and establish the kingdom of God on earth. Jesus tells them the kingdom of God is like a seed planted in the ground. Once planted, God gives it growth without the sower ever knowing how. Just as it is God who gives growth to nature, so it is God who will give growth to the Church. The Christian's task is simply to plant the seed and be faithful, then trust in God to do the rest. This is precisely what happened in the early Church. It was the example of the first Christians, particularly their love for each other, that God used to draw countless others to accept Jesus and his way. The movement grew beyond everyone's imagining like a snowball rolling down a hill of newly fallen snow. It culminated eventually in the conversion to Christianity of the vast Roman Empire.

The parable of the mustard seed was intended to assure the early Church of eventual success. Its point was to show that even though the number of faithful followers might initially be few, God would ultimately see to its increase. And so it happened. From twelve uneducated men, the Church did in fact spread to the whole known world, winning over even princes and kings.

Calming the Sea

The sea plays a prominent part in the first half of Mark's Gospel. The Gospel opens with Jesus calling his first four disciples as he walks along the Sea of Galilee. He also spends considerable time crisscrossing the same sea as he moves from shore to shore teaching, preaching, and healing people of every manner of infirmity (Mk 5-7). His first nature miracle, the calming of the sea, which we read of in today's Gospel, likewise takes place on the Sea of Galilee, as does his most impressive early theophany or revelation of his divinity, which takes place when Jesus walks upon the water (Mk 6:45-52). For a commentary on Matthew's account of same, cf. the Nineteenth Sunday of the year in Cycle A.

The Sea of Galilee is an inland body of water stretching twelve miles from north to south and six miles from east to west. It forms part of the eastern border of Galilee (hence Matthew and Mark call it the Sea of Galilee), but on its western shore lies the great city of Tiberias and the Plain of Gennesaret (hence John calls it the Sea of Tiberias and Luke calls it the Lake of Gennesaret). It is a fresh water body that lies 685 feet below the level of the Mediterranean Sea and it is almost completely surrounded by mountains. The clash in temperatures between the cool air from the mountain peaks and the warm air shimmering above the low-lying surface of the water can create sudden, violent storms with little or no warning. The topography of the area further intensifies the storms. While the sea is completely blocked by mountains on the east, there is a break in the Mt. Carmel range to the west. Wind from the west funnels through the mountain gap and intensifies in speed as it does so. It then sweeps over the relatively shallow water, churning it up, until it slams into the solid mountain range to the east. There it is deflected and sent back over the same body of water from the opposite direction, adding to the turbulence of an already violent sea.

Today's Gospel episode, together with Jesus' walking on the water, were particularly dear to the early Church. To understand why, we should understand something of the cosmology or perceived world order in ancient Palestine. The ancient Jews believed God inhabited the heavens. The sky was his fiefdom, his domain. Humankind inhabited the earth. God had given us dominion over it. But there was one part of the earth beyond human control: the sea. The ancient Hebrews were terrified of the sea. It could rise up without warning and swallow ships and sailors alike. It could overwhelm and smash the mightiest vessels and send their occupants to a watery grave. The sea, they concluded, was the abode of the devil and his evil spirits. They were powerless against it. As the abode of the devil, only God could master the sea and subdue it. Psalm 89:10 proclaims God indeed has the power to control the sea, and Job (9:8) reminds us God alone can tread upon the towering crests of the sea.

With a clearer understanding of the Jewish attitude towards the sea in New Testament times, we can better appreciate why today's Gospel of Jesus taming the sea and Mark 6:45-52 where Jesus walks upon the water were of such vital importance to the early Church. They marked the clearest manifestation of the divinity of Jesus prior to the resurrection. Jesus calmed the sea with a simple command and it obeyed him. If the sea is the abode of the devil and only God can control the sea and the devil, in calming the sea Jesus incontrovertibly demonstrated truly divine power. In walking upon the raging sea, a prerogative limited to God alone, Jesus further proved his divinity. While the Apostles did not fully comprehend this until after the resurrection, they at least started to pose the right type of question, "Who then is this whom even wind and sea obey?" With hindsight gained from the resurrection, however, the early Church more fully appreciated the significance of the events and cherished them accordingly.

In today's Gospel Mark tells us Jesus "rebuked" the wind and told the sea to be "quiet." These are the very same words he used to drive out the unclean spirits from the unfortunate man (Mark 1:25): "Jesus rebuked him and said, 'Quiet! Come out of him!'" (cf. Fourth Sunday of the Year, Cycle B). Mark highlights the same choice of words to remind his readers that in calming the sea as well as in ridding the hapless fellow of the unclean spirits bedeviling him, Jesus clearly showed mastery over Satan and the power of evil. In doing so, Jesus continued to advance and strengthen the kingdom of God on earth by further weakening Satan's power in the world and routing his minions from previously secure bases.

The importance to the early Church of Jesus' calming of the sea and walking on the waves is also evidenced by how they helped to shape the early Church's vision of itself. As witnessed in early Christian art, a favorite image of early believers depicted the Church as the bark of St. Peter. They were on the sea of life, trying to get to the heavenly shore, but constantly tossed about and threatened by evil forces and cruel persecutions. From the calming of the sea episode, they concluded that even though Jesus seemed distant or asleep, they had no need to fear if they put their faith in him. From the account of Jesus' walking on the waves, they came to realize as long as Jesus was within the Church, the bark of Peter, neither the forces of evil nor the gates of hell could prevail against it. They came away so galvanized and confident that despite terribly trying circumstances including the Roman arena, they were able to keep the faith and eventually bring about the conversion of their persecutors and their empire.

The Daughter of Jairus and the Woman
with the Hemorrhages

Today's Gospel is from Mark. Mark's primary concern in the first part of his Gospel is to show Jesus is a prophet powerful in word and deed. The ordinary people recognize this at once because "he taught them as one having authority and not as the scribes" (1:22) and "he commands even the unclean spirits and they obey him" (1:27). The scribes and Pharisees, however, are quick to take exception to Jesus' activity (2:7, 2:16, 2:24, 3:6) and soon accuse him of being the devil's pawn (3:22). Mark then proceeds to show Jesus is mightier even than Satan himself and all the forces of evil.

In last week's Gospel Mark presented Jesus calming the sea (Mk 4:35-41). The sea was considered the abode of the devil and only God could calm the sea. With a simple command, "Quiet, be still," Jesus calmed the sea and brought peace out of chaos, thereby clearly demonstrating to the Jewish world that Jesus was more powerful than Satan. In today's Gospel Mark presents Jesus casting out sickness and death, the effects of original sin, which Jewish theology also associated with the power of the devil and his demons. Sick people at the time were thought to be in the hands of Satan. In curing a woman from sickness and raising a young girl from the dead, the effects of sin which Satan brought into the world, Jesus again demonstrates he is more powerful than Satan for he wrests people from his dominion and domination.

Here Mark uses an ancient storytelling technique of splitting up one story and sandwiching it or bracketing it around another story to highlight and enhance similarities or contrasts. He inserts the story of the woman with the hemorrhages in the middle of the story of the daughter of Jairus. Note the stories' similarities: both involve women; both illustrate the need for faith and confidence in Jesus; both involve a deed or touch; both women are called daughter; the girl is 12 years old, the woman has been sick for 12 years. Besides highlighting the similarities, splitting the Jairus story adds tension and suspense to this far more dramatic and extraordinary miracle by delaying its ultimate conclusion of final resuscitation till the end.

If we consider each story separately without interruption, we see Jairus, a synagogue official and therefore a prominent Jewish leader, approach Jesus with a request to cure his daughter. Given the open hostility to Jesus on the part of the scribes and Pharisees cited above, this was a bold and courageous move, suggesting an open and independent mind and, more importantly, deep faith and trust in Jesus. As they make their way to his house, Jesus is delayed by his search among the crowd for the woman who touched him, thus, according to Mark's rendition of the story, putting the anxious and understandably upset father to a still deeper test of faith. Before they can resume their journey, the distraught father's faith is tested yet again, this time to the breaking point. Servants from the house arrive announcing it is too late, the little girl is dead.

Up to this point Jesus has raised no one from the dead, something almost unimaginable at the time. But when Jesus tells Jairus to have faith, he holds up remarkably and proceeds to follow Jesus. His faith remains unshaken even when Jesus is greeted with ridicule by the crowd made up of neighbors, relatives, and friends. The house is in uproar from mourning, with keening and wailing as is typical in the Mideast, just as earlier the sea was an uproar of wind and waves. Jesus stills the crowd as he stilled the sea, in this case by putting them all out of the house. Then taking the little girl's hand, with a single command as with the sea, he restores her to life. *Talitha koum*: Little girl, I say to you, arise!

Earlier the servants referred to Jesus as "teacher." Unlike the Matthean usage where "teacher" is invariably employed by outsiders of Jesus as a mark of derision or disdain, "teacher" in Mark always signifies respect and is Mark's way of indicating that Jesus is about to reveal something important. Here Jesus teaches not in word but in deed by revealing through his action that he has power over death, a prerogative reserved to God alone.

The second story is about a woman who, though only sick, was as good as dead. Because of an irregular cycle, she was considered unclean by rabbinical law. Her condition made difficult or impossible marriage, motherhood, even ordinary social contact. Anyone coming in contact with her was also rendered unclean (Lv 15:25-27). That's why she sneaks up behind Jesus and touches not his person but only the hem of his garment. Yet her faith in Jesus and his power to heal her is enormous and it carries the day. Jesus feels power go out from him and she is immediately cured.

Jesus then searches the crowd to discern who touched him. The woman steps forward and in confessing what happened professes her profound faith in Jesus. Jesus then assures her before the whole crowd that her faith has *cured* her, using a deliberate double entendre that also means *saved* her. Jesus thus suggests that the woman has been restored to far more than physical well being. Her faith in Jesus has also set her right with God. In curing sickness which entered the world through sin and which the ancient Jewish world believed to be akin to possession by the devil, Jesus once again demonstrates he is more powerful than Satan and sin.

Much more than merely relating past history, the Gospels as written by the evangelists proclaim what God can continue to do in the world through faith in Jesus. Let us pray that we who also know illness in our lives and experience grief for deceased loved ones will have something of the faith of Jairus and the woman with the hemorrhages so that God may also heal us both spiritually and physically.

Rejection of God's Elect: Jesus, Paul, and Ezekiel

A common theme running through all three readings for today is rejection. If we start first with the Gospel and work backwards through the readings, we see Jesus return home to his small town of Nazareth after considerable success in the larger city of Capernaum and its environs only to be rejected by his own kith and kin. This Gospel passage comes from a section of Mark in which the miracle stories are connected by a mutual link between family and faith that is common to them all. It starts in 3:31-35 where Jesus explains to his followers that his *real* family is not comprised of mother, brothers, or sisters but of everyone who does the will of God. In short, the family of God is not determined by biological connections but by obedience to God's will.

In three subsequent miracles reference to family and faith plays prominently. When Jesus cures the man with an unclean spirit, he sends him back to his family to stir up their faith by telling them what the Lord had done for him (5:1-20). In the story of the daughter of Jairus, Jesus restores the girl to life in response to the father's great faith and then immediately reintroduces the girl back into family life by suggesting her parents give her something to eat (5:35-43). In curing the woman with the hemorrhages, Jesus addresses her as "daughter" and declares her faith has cured her (5:25-34).

With this background emphasizing the close connection between faith and family, Jesus arrives back at Nazareth, his hometown, where he would have many cousins and extended family members. He has already achieved wide prominence and recognition in other parts of Galilee (1:28). Now he begins to teach in their synagogue and they are astonished. Those who are true followers, his *real* family, sense that God is present in Jesus and his words. The ordinary people of Nazareth, however, many of whom were members of his extended biological family, never even dreamed of the presence of God in one they (thought they) knew so well. They could put no faith in one of their own whom they thought was just like they were and sadly they rejected him. In many ways this passage serves as a microcosm of the overall Gospel. Jesus came to his own, the Jewish people, and they too rejected him. By a tragic quirk of fate, it appeared easier for Gentiles and foreigners to put faith in Jesus than it was for his own people.

In the second reading from Second Corinthians, Paul also intimates that he too was rejected. Here he speaks of a thorn in his side. Earlier speculation centered on some form of temptation of the flesh but modern Scripture scholarship suggests Paul is referring to a group of malcontents in Corinth who were maligning him and trying to undermine his apostolic ministry and effectiveness (2 Cor 11). Paul, who also felt the sting of rejection, concludes by rejoicing for he knows the more his inadequacies are exposed, the more evident it will be that God is responsible for whatever good is accomplished in his ministry.

The first reading tells of the prophetic call of Ezekiel. God warns Ezekiel from the very start that he will face rejection. As the Israelites rebelled against God and their fathers revolted against his ways, so Ezekiel can expect they will react to him when he brings them God's message. Yet he must stand firm to let the people know a prophet of God is among them. God then gives Ezekiel a scroll and tells him to eat it, a sign that he has internalized God's message and made it his own. Finally God warns him once again that the people will not listen.

Ezekiel began his work as a prophet in the first Babylonian exile (597 BC) prior to the fall of Jerusalem and the second wave of exiles (587 BC). Like Jeremiah with whom he overlapped in time, Ezekiel had to prophesy doom for Jerusalem. But unlike Jeremiah who hoped the people would repent in time to forestall destruction, Ezekiel was convinced it was too late and God's wrath was inevitable. A spectacular series of visions (chs. 8-11) had persuaded him Jerusalem was corrupt to the core. The subsequent destruction of Jerusalem, which verified his earlier prophecies, happened to coincide with the death of Ezekiel's wife. As a prophetic sign God forbade him to mourn her in order to show the exiles they were not to grieve for their vanquished city. Then, with their punishment complete and their capital obliterated, Ezekiel's message changed suddenly and completely from words of doom to words of hope.

To the swelled number of exiles from the second and final banishment after the destruction of Jerusalem, he offered new insight into God's plan. He assured them they would always be God's chosen people. He explained it was because of their covenant violations that they had been punished. But once purified, he promised God would give them a new heart and a new spirit, a heart of flesh and not of stone so they would keep his laws. For the sake of his own holiness, God would deliver them and restore them to the land that was sacred to their fathers. They would be God's people and Yahweh would be their God (Ezk 36:23-29). Their enemies in turn would feel the full fury of God against them (Ezk 25-32), while God would set up his sanctuary among his people and remain with them forever (Ezk 37:27). As the prophets before him, Ezekiel stressed the interior nature of religion, the reality of sin, personal responsibility for sin, and the inexorability of God's punishment for sin. He differed from his predecessors, however, in ending with considerably greater emphasis on the Temple and cultic observances (Ezk 40-48). For this he has often been called the "father of Judaism."

The common theme of rejection that pervades today's readings is no cause for depression. It is offset by the power of God which will ultimately prevail despite human weakness. Like St. Paul, let us rejoice in our weakness and take comfort and confidence in God's strength.

Sending Out the Twelve

In today's Gospel Jesus sends out the twelve Apostles to share in the work of evangelization. Limited in his human body by the conditions of time and space, he seeks the help of his companions in bringing to completion the mission given him by his Father. His injunction to his disciples is reminiscent of Old Testament times. The great prophet Elisha commissioned his assistant Gehazi to share in his ministry of healing in similar fashion: "Gird your loins, take my staff with you and be off; if you meet anyone, do not greet him, and if anyone greets you, do not answer" (2 K 4:29). Elisha's final command, though not mentioned explicitly in Mark, is recorded in Luke (10:4). It is intended to lend a note of urgency to the completion of God's mission and task. Mark captures this need for urgency in his rendition of Jesus' commissioning of his Apostles by stressing no time can be spared for gathering food, clothing, or money—things that would otherwise be considered essential.

Besides emphasizing the need for urgency, the deliberate omission of even the bare basics from the upcoming missionary endeavor is intended to drive home to all those commissioned the true source of any eventual success. It is a subtle yet strong reminder to the Apostles and the early Church alike that true apostolic success in evangelization comes solely from the power of God and is in no way contingent on the personal position, power, or prestige of the messenger. The radical call to jettison even basic essentials to expedite the mission is also intended as a challenge to the Apostles and all subsequent missionaries to exercise profound faith in God, such as they will ask of those they encounter in calling them to conversion. The concluding reference to shaking the dust from their feet is an ominous warning that like the prophets before them and Jesus himself, they will encounter rejection in pursuing God's will.

Mark Link, S.J. offers an interesting connection between today's Gospel and St. Francis of Assisi (*Illustrated Sunday Homilies,* Series 1, Year B, p. 81). St. Francis of Assisi (1182-1226) was the son of affluent Italian parents. His youth was given over largely to parties and pleasure with a claque of ne'er-do-well friends whom he helped to support with his considerable income. When hostilities broke out between Assisi and Perugia in 1202, however, things changed dramatically. Francis joined the forces of Assisi and galloped off to war. There he was captured by Perugia and confined to a dark, dank dungeon. Released in broken health after a year of confinement, it took him another full year to regain his strength.

The deprivations of prison and the uncertainties of convalescence completely changed Francis' outlook on life. He abandoned his worldly ways and fancy clothes for the lifestyle and attire of a peasant. He left his comfortable home and moved into a decrepit, tumbled down old church at the edge of Assisi where he assumed the life of a hermit. There he spent his time alone in prayer and meditation on Sacred Scripture. His reflections on Scripture led him to a deep love and concern for the poor and socially less desirable. Two Bible passages in particular pushed him in this direction. The first, from Genesis (1:27), speaks of every person being created in the image and likeness of God. The second, from Matthew (25:45), guarantees that whatever we do for the least of Jesus' brothers and sisters, that we do for him.

Despite the impact of Scripture on his life, Francis might well have remained a hermit living in isolation were it not for the Gospel passage we read at Mass today. One day at Mass, he heard this very same Gospel segment read and it changed his life forever. Moved by Jesus' command to go forth to push back the forces of evil and preach the need for repentance, he felt he could no longer remain a hermit cut off from the world. Especially compelling was the urgency with which Jesus expected his disciples to respond to his call, allowing no time or concern for material provisions as basic as food, clothing, or money. In God's enterprise, one was to trust totally in God. In response, Francis opted for extreme poverty in all his future missionary endeavors.

Francis then set out, a poor vagabond, to preach the word of God throughout Italy. The infectious nature of his personality and the urgency of his cause quickly attracted other generous young people. Soon an army of followers was on the march. Often with no place to lay their heads, they survived simply on what the people they ministered to gave them. Three years short of thirty, Francis got permission from the Pope to establish a religious order. Franciscans were to love poverty as a mother and devote themselves tirelessly to working for the poor. Today eight hundred years later thousands of Franciscan priests, brothers, sisters, and associates continue the tradition of St. Francis and give their lives selflessly in the service of God's poor.

Just as St. Francis was called by today's Gospel passage to service, so are we. We are called to drive out the evil spirits of racism, selfishness, and prejudice in ourselves and our society. We are called to heal, to heal the bereaved, the rejected, the depressed, the overwhelmed among our families, friends, and neighbors. We are called to preach the good news of God's love for us, not necessarily in words but by the love we manifest in our lives. We are to trust in God and not worry about material things, recalling God was able to fashion us, the pinnacle of all creation, out of nothing but spit and mud.

Sheep Without a Shepherd

The more I read Mark, the more amazed I am at how tightly his Gospel is structured and how carefully he organized every little detail to highlight the message and purpose of Jesus and his teaching. Today's Gospel passage, for example, seems at first glance little more than a transition between the Gospel segment we read last week and the one scheduled to be read next week. But a closer reading of the text reveals that Mark carefully uses today's Gospel passage to put into perspective what happened in last week's Gospel and to set the stage for what will occur in next week's Gospel.

Last week we read about Jesus sending the Apostles out in groups of two to preach the need for repentance and share in his ministry of healing. An intervening passage, not included in the lectionary for Sunday readings, records the death of John the Baptist and is structurally part of today's Gospel segment. Mark uses the shocking report of John's brutal beheading to cast new light on the Apostles' mission. The Apostles were sent to preach repentance, just as John was. Like John, they were to preach it in season and out of season. The jarring news of John's murder, then, serves as a stunning reminder that preaching God's message can be dangerous, spreading God's word can lead to the Cross. When powerful people like Herod prove unwilling to hear or to heed, God's messengers can be hurt. It is a warning of what may come, of what can be asked of God's emissaries, just as it will be asked of Jesus himself. Mark's reference to John's martyrdom, in short, is intended to remove part of the glow from the Apostles' earlier successful missionary endeavors and alert them to the possibility of dire things to come. It is a strong yet subtle reminder that they should neither expect nor seek unrelieved success and triumph as disciples of Jesus.

Today's Gospel also sets the background against which to

understand next week's Gospel. In the next section of Mark we encounter the multiplication of loaves and fish. On the surface level today's Gospel explains why such a large number of people happened to be in a deserted place where they occasioned and benefited from one of Jesus' most spectacular miracles. The crowds had earlier been fascinated by Jesus' teaching and when he set sail with his Apostles across the lake toward an isolated region on the opposite shore in search of a respite, they simply scurried around the lake on foot and intercepted him. Importuned by their numbers and dogged persistence, Jesus graciously abandons his plans for a much needed rest and immediately resumes teaching them.

On a far deeper level, however, Mark uses today's Gospel passage to highlight scriptural parallels with the Old Testament. Mark tells us that Jesus looked with pity on the crowd who were like "sheep without a shepherd," a thinly veiled reference to Moses who before his death asked God to send someone to take his place and lead the people, precisely so they would not end up as "sheep without a shepherd" (Nb 27:17). To help his reader understand the significance of the upcoming miraculous multiplication of loaves and fish, Mark uses the scriptural shepherd allusion and the deserted location in today's Gospel segment to suggest Jesus is the long awaited successor of Moses. Jesus will not only lead his people but also feed them with bread that is far superior to the manna which Moses managed to obtain for them during their exodus in the desert (Ex 16). Mark has already shown that Jesus has power over the sea (Mk 6:45-52), similar to the power Moses exercised over the Red Sea (Ex 14:21). Mark has also reported that Jesus enjoys great renown as a teacher, that he is respected as one who teaches with authority (Mk 1:27), a further similarity to Moses long considered the greatest teacher and lawgiver of the Old Testament. In evoking these Old Testament images, today's Gospel passage sets the tone for next week's Gospel and invites the reader to see in the upcoming multiplication of loaves and fish that Jesus is not only the successor of Moses but also shares in the charisma and mission of Moses.

Later through the use of almost identical language patterns he will tie the multiplication of loaves to the even more wondrous, faith-challenging institution of the Eucharist (Mk 14:22-24). The shepherd image that Jesus uses in today's Gospel is common through all of Scripture. It conveys the notion of leading and nurturing and is used frequently for God and the kings and leaders of the Jewish people. Ezekiel was particularly fond of the reverse image of a bad shepherd to describe the conduct of the rulers in his day, people who fed themselves and not their flocks, who failed to provide leadership and allowed the people to fall victim to predators who led them away from their faith (Ezk 34). In today's first reading Jeremiah uses a similar image, calling down God's wrath on those who mislead and scatter the flock and fail to provide proper leadership and guidance. The kings' interest in forging foreign alliances all too often led to pagan practices permeating the whole country. Jeremiah prophesies here that God will raise up true shepherds to help his people in their present need while one day establishing a righteous king, a shoot of Jesse, who will govern (shepherd) wisely.

The lamentable theme of sheep without a shepherd straying from God's ways, so common in Scripture, is equally applicable in our day. We find it everywhere: the unabating hatred, and distrust, and violence in the Middle East and Northern Ireland, the boiling tensions in the Balkans, the internecine wars and slaughter in Rwanda, Burundi, Congo, Angola, and Sierra Leone. Let us ask God to send us world leaders who will help us find our way back to peace and justice so all can live in harmony and peace.

The Multiplication of the Loaves and Fish

The multiplication of the loaves and fish is the subject of today's Gospel. This event constitutes one of the most important and highly regarded miracles of Our Lord in the eyes of the early and modern Church. It is the only miracle of Jesus recorded in all four Gospels and the only miracle assigned as a Sunday reading in each of the three cycles of the new liturgical year. Since this particular passage comes from John, let us see how the miracle fits into the overall structure of John's Gospel and how John uses the event to advance his own theological message and perspective. Today's Gospel, by the way, marks the first of four consecutive Sunday readings from John 6, known as the Eucharistic chapter.

The miraculous multiplication of loaves and fish we read of today is one of only seven miracles that John includes in his Gospel to reveal who Jesus truly is. The miracle of the loaves and fish supports a major theme of the Fourth Gospel: Jesus is the way to eternal life. John begins by telling us Jesus crossed the Sea of Galilee to the shore of Tiberias to escape the crowds. There he ascended a mountain to be alone with his disciples. In Scripture a mountain is typically the place where revelation from God takes place. Here in particular John uses it to summon up images of Moses on Mt. Sinai (Ex 19).

John next points out that the Jewish feast of Passover was near. Mere mention of Passover would be sufficient to remind his readers who were well versed in Scripture of the great leader Moses. It was Moses who led the Jewish people from the slavery of Egypt to the freedom of the Promised Land. During their forty-year trek through the desert Moses also managed to provide for their physical needs with bread from heaven in the form of manna at dawn and quail from the sky at dusk. The setting, then, is designed to help the reader discover that Jesus is the new Moses, one designated by

God to lead all people safely to the kingdom of heaven.

The action begins with Jesus asking Philip where they can buy bread to feed all the people they see streaming towards them in the hope of benefiting from the power of Jesus' teaching and cures. Philip was from Bethsaida, a small fishing village on the other side of the Sea of Galilee, and Jesus may have thought Philip would know something of the cost of food along the lake. Philip concludes immediately and correctly that it would be impossible to feed such a huge crowd even with two hundred days' wages, thus putting the magnitude of the upcoming miracle into proper perspective.

Meanwhile all the Apostles have been able to scout up is five barley loaves and a couple of fish. Barley is hardier than wheat and matures faster, ripening in early spring, in time for Passover. Mention of the barley loaves sets today's miracle against the backdrop of our first reading (2 K 4:42-44), in which Elisha miraculously feeds 100 men with 20 loaves, a major Old Testament miracle that nonetheless pales before Jesus' feeding of 5000 people with 5 loaves. In both accounts there are leftovers, a rare phenomenon in a near subsistence economy, indicating that the largesse has clearly come from God. The leftovers fill twelve baskets, an important number in both the Old and the New Testaments. As God provided enough food to feed the original twelve tribes of Israel during their exodus through the desert so, John suggests, God will now furnish sufficient food to feed the new Israel founded on the twelve Apostles.

Having witnessed this spectacular feeding of a horde of over 5000 people, the crowd begins to speak of Jesus as the prophet who is to come into the world, correctly identifying him as the prophet Moses prayed would succeed him (Dt 18:15). But carried away by their pressing material needs at the moment and hopeful of even greater political and economic benefits to follow, the only thing the crowd can think of is seizing Jesus right then and there and forcing him to become king. To preserve the integrity of his mission, Jesus is compelled to flee back to the mountain alone.

Besides looking back to the Old Testament and highlighting similarities between Jesus and Moses, John's account of the multiplication of loaves and fish also sheds penetrating light on the New Testament and offers rich Eucharistic insights. The miraculous multiplication of food took place around Passover. Jesus instituted the Eucharist at the Last Supper, a meal commemorating the Passover. Also, according to John's account, it is Jesus himself, and not his disciples, who distributes the food to the crowd, just as later it is Jesus who personally distributes the bread and wine to his disciples at the Last Supper. Before distributing the loaves and fish, Jesus has the crowd recline, the same position people assumed to eat the Passover meal and the same position the Apostles assumed at the Last Supper (Jn 13:23).

While John alone does not mention the institution of the Eucharist at the Last Supper, all three other evangelists do. They are also closely united in reporting nearly identical formulas for the words Jesus used to change the bread and wine into his body and blood. Common to all the formulas recorded for the institution of the Eucharist are the words: took, blessed or gave thanks, broke, and gave. Three or all four of these very same words are also used in all four Gospel accounts of the miraculous feeding of the 5000. Besides linking Jesus and his mission back to the great Old Testament prophets like Moses and Elisha, then, the multiplication of the loaves and fish was clearly intended to strengthen the faith of the Apostles and early Church in the power of Jesus to institute the Eucharist. If Jesus had the power to multiply bread and fish physically so as to satisfy the hunger of a huge crowd, then it was also possible he had the power to change bread and wine into his body and blood as food he promised to prepare his followers and preserve them for everlasting life.

Manna in the Desert

The first reading for today from Exodus is about manna, the miraculous bread with which God fed the Jewish people during their forty years of wandering in the desert in search of the Promised Land. Manna also features prominently in John's presentation of the Bread of Life Discourse which we begin in today's Gospel and will continue to read for the next two weeks. Since manna is an important concept in both the Old and New Testaments, it might be good to say something about it today. While the Bread of Life Discourse is also particularly beautiful and critically important, we shall save comment on it for two weeks until we have finished reading the entire discourse. We will then be in a better position to view the discourse as a literary whole and draw distinctions and contrasts between the sections assigned to the different Sundays.

The setting for today's first reading is the Sinai desert where the Jewish people fled after God had rescued them from the hands of the Egyptians in a series of dramatic and heart-stopping episodes. Despite the many wonders they had witnessed God perform on their behalf, they still found it difficult to trust God and adjust to the new surroundings God had placed them in. Forgetting all the horrors they endured in captivity in Egypt, they focused and fixated solely on the food they had enjoyed in the fertile regions along the Nile and began to grumble about their current conditions. Not daring to criticize Yahweh directly, they leveled their complaints against Yahweh's representatives, Moses and Aaron, accusing them of leading them into the desert to starve.

Once again out of pity for his people, or this time perhaps for Moses and Aaron who had to put up with their constant carping, God intervenes and sends manna. In Exodus (16:13-15) we are told that when the morning dew evaporated, fine flakes like hoarfrost lay on the ground. The flakes were like coriander seeds, but white, and tasted like a wafer made with honey. According to Numbers

(11:8) the people ground them up and made them into loaves that tasted like cakes made with oil. The name manna is said to come from the Hebrew *man hu*, which means, "What is this?" (Ex 16:15).

Manna is a substance that is still found in the Sinai Peninsula today, though in minute quantities. It consists of small, white kernels formed from the droplets of sap that fall from the tamarisk tree when insects tap into its bark. Thus God used something perfectly natural to feed his people. What was miraculous was the amount of manna provided, enough to feed all the people all the time, and the regularity with which it appeared, each and every day, with a double portion on the eve of the Sabbath to obviate the need for Sabbath work. Each person was directed to gather no more than was needed for himself and his dependents. The one who gathered more found he had not too much, the one who gathered less found he had not too little. No one was to keep it for the next day. Anyone trying to do so found it foul and full of maggots. On the eve of the Sabbath, however, all were to gather a double portion to preclude work on the Sabbath. Miraculously the second portion did not sour or rot over the Sabbath eve. Anyone seeking new manna on the Sabbath was inevitably disappointed. None ever appeared (Ex 16:16-28). The manna never once failed the people in their wanderings in the desert. It ceased only after the Jews had crossed the Jordan and could live off the bounty of the Promised Land (Jos 5:12). As a tribute to Yahweh and a reminder to future generations, Moses ordered an urn of manna placed before the Ark of the Covenant to serve as a perpetual memorial (Ex 16:32-36).

While God's gift of manna has dominated both the Old and New Testament recollections of divine intervention during the critical period of the Exodus, from a historical point of view quail was also very much part and parcel of God's original beneficence. The Jewish people had complained of the lack of both bread (Ex 16:3) and meat (Nb 11:4), so God was careful to provide them with a daily ration of quail as well as bread. Like the manna, the quail God provided can also be explained in natural and supernatural terms.

Huge flocks of quail are known to have migrated between Europe and Africa over the Sinai Peninsula in ancient times. The phenomenon has been recorded in secular history by Herodotus, Aristotle, and Pliny. Often the quail simply dropped to the ground exhausted from their flight, where they were easily caught and immensely enjoyed. While their numbers have been severely decimated over time, Egypt continued to export more than two million of them a year as late as 1920.

What was miraculous during the time of the Exodus was the vast number of birds that descended in the vicinity of the Jewish camp and the regularity with which they continued to come even outside the usual migratory season. The Jewish people never again had cause to complain about a lack of meat during their desert sojourn. Quail routinely descended on the camp each evening, enough to feed the entire people. The Book of Numbers (11:31-34) even reports an untoward incident in which the Hebrew wanderers abused the abundance of quail to overindulge their appetites. While their mouths were still filled with the meat, God's anger flared against them and struck them with a severe plague.

The story of God feeding his people with manna in the desert is found in the earliest Old Testament traditions and manuscripts and it has never lost its luster. By New Testament times when the Jewish people were longing for the coming of the Messiah, they began to think of manna as the food of messianic times. It is this that the people have in mind in today's Gospel when they ask for a sign. They are hoping that if Jesus is the Messiah, as they suspect he is, he will give them manna to eat and thereby issue in a time of prosperity and plenty for all.

As we start the Bread of Life Discourse and reflect on God's generous gift of manna to sustain the Jewish people physically during their journey through the desert in search of the Promised Land, let us remember that God has given us much more. On the night before he died, Jesus instituted the Eucharist to help and nourish us spiritually in our pilgrimage through life in quest of heaven.

Elijah

The Gospel for the Nineteenth Sunday of the Year continues the Bread of Life Discourse from last week. It expands on the themes we developed for the Eighteenth Sunday of the Year. Today's first reading from the First Book of Kings (19:4-8) deals with Elijah. Since we rarely get a chance to talk about this great prophet, it might be good to take a look at his life and activity today. Unlike the later prophets who are remembered mainly from their writings, Elijah left no written records behind. His life and activity were recorded by others in the First Book of Kings.

In 1 Kings 19:4 we read Elijah is at a very low ebb and praying for death. The setting is during the reign of Ahab, the most abominable and loathsome king of Israel. As 1 Kings 16:33 reports, "He did more to anger the Lord, the God of Israel, than any of the kings of Israel before him." For purely political reasons Ahab decided to marry the Phoenician princess Jezebel who brazenly arrived in Israel with a retinue replete with the pagan gods and prophets of her people. The latter quickly established places of worship for Baal where, to please his foreign wife and curry favor with the powerful princes of Phoenicia, Ahab shamelessly shared in their pagan sacrifices. In doing so, he caused considerable consternation and disedification among his people.

Baal was a god of fertility, worshipped mainly to bring about an increase in crop yields, usually by delivering rain. The Canaanites were far more advanced in the ways of agriculture than their formerly nomadic Jewish neighbors and hence also more productive. The largely uneducated Jewish peasants were well aware of the harvest differentials. They could spell the difference between subsistence and starvation for farmers struggling on small plots. But given the superstitions and sketchy scientific knowledge at the time, the Jews were never quite sure whether the Phoenician advantage was due to better agricultural techniques or their devotion to Baal. The latter they worshipped under the guise of a young bull, the symbol par excellence for fertility in the ancient world. To counter this insidious slide into syncretism away from Israel's strict monotheism, Elijah, the only prophet of Yahweh left in Israel, single-handedly dared challenge the hundreds of prophets of Baal in the most dramatic contest ever recorded in the Old Testament.

At a time of deep and prolonged drought, Elijah proposed that each side offer a sacrifice to its respective deity to determine which was the true God. By agreement the prophets of Baal were the first to prepare their sacrifice. They then danced around as part of their customary ritual and asked Baal to show his mighty power by consuming their sacrifice. But despite their dervish dancing and their lashing of themselves till they bled profusely, nothing happened. Meanwhile Elijah kept taunting them with unshakable confidence. He suggested sardonically that they call louder, for their god might be sleeping, or meditating, or even away on a journey.

When Elijah's turn came, he prepared his sacrifice and three times doused it with water till the water filled the surrounding trench to overflowing. Only then did he call upon Yahweh who instantly consumed his sacrifice and the surrounding water with fire. Thereupon the heavens opened and a deluge of much-needed rain poured from the sky. With Yahweh convincingly and overwhelmingly demonstrating superiority over Baal, Elijah seized the initiative and summarily ordered the execution of all the 450 prophets of Baal in the land (1 K 18:20-46). In doing so, Elijah removed a grave threat to the monotheism of his people but brought far greater personal danger on himself.

Elijah's success and impertinence infuriated Jezebel and sent her into a furious rage. She swiftly vowed vengeance and he was forced to flee for his life. He knew well what she was capable of, for she had already eliminated all of Yahweh's prophets except himself. It is here that today's story picks up. An angel of the Lord brings Elijah food and sends him on a journey of forty days through the desert to Mt. Horeb in search of God and his message. Here we see an unmistakable parallel with Moses. Mt. Horeb is but another name for Mt. Sinai, the same mountain to which God had earlier summoned Moses. There God had met with Moses during the Israelites' forty years of wandering through the desert and revealed to him the Ten Commandments. Moses, too, had once pleaded for death, when overwhelmed by the intransigence of his own people during the Exodus (Nb 11:15). Through his angel intermediary sent to Elijah, God demonstrates his willingness to help his chosen people in whatever crisis they face just as he helped the original Israelites when they needed assistance in the desert.

Elijah eats the food as he is bidden and forty days later arrives safely at a cave on the top of Mt. Horeb. There in one of the loveliest stories in the Old Testament he encounters God not in a mighty wind, nor in an earthquake, nor in a fire, but in a gentle breeze (1 K 19:11-13). Here, like Moses, he is enlightened about his responsibility as a prophet and leader of God's people. Elijah is given three divine commissions, two of which involve stirring up rebellions to unseat forever Ahab's line, the House of Omri, that had doggedly and despicably tried to divert the people from the true worship and service of Yahweh. Scripture scholars suggest that God's point in summoning Elijah to the top of Mt. Horeb following a forty days journey through the Sinai desert suggests that the essence of the prophetic movement and message involved nothing more than a call for a pilgrimage back to Sinai, a return to Israel's original faith experience.

Elijah's third assignment was concerned with the Naboth affair in which Elijah called Ahab to task for unlawfully seizing land at the cost of an innocent Israelite life (1 K 21). Ahab wanted Naboth's vineyard for a vegetable garden but Naboth would not part with his ancestral land. So Jezebel arranged to have trumped up charges brought against Naboth that led to his stoning. The story is designed to provide a window or opening into the social side of the prophetic mission, the other major thrust or priority of the prophet's message. In short, the prophets, of whom Elijah was one of the first and greatest, were called not only to summon the people back to their original faith in God but also to remind them of their communal duties to others in justice and charity.

Conclusion of the Bread of Life Discourse

Today's Gospel is the conclusion of the Bread of Life of Discourse which we have read over the past three Sundays. Let's start by first locating the passage in John's Gospel. Then we can say something about the overall discourse itself.

The Bread of Life Discourse is situated in the first half of John's Gospel called the Book of Signs. John typically calls the miracles of Jesus signs because they show forth or *sign*ify God's power at work in Jesus. Of all the signs or miracles that Jesus worked in his lifetime, John finds room for only seven in his Gospel. In each instance he first records the sign or miracle itself and then follows it immediately with a discourse in which Jesus then explains the meaning of the miracle or shows the "significance" of the sign. In John's Gospel the Bread of Life Discourse is the teaching Jesus offers to explain the multiplication of the loaves and fish which immediately preceded it.

In that miracle Jesus wondrously feeds over 5000 people with an amazingly few loaves and fish. Soon after the crowds are back looking for more. Jesus is disappointed because they completely missed the significance of the event. He had performed the miracle to bolster their faith in him and to show he was greater than Elisha who had fed 100 men with 20 barley loaves during a severe famine (2 K 4:42-44). At the same time he also demonstrated he was greater than Moses who had fed their ancestors with manna that God sent from heaven while they wandered for forty years in the desert.

Another reason Jesus multiplied bread physically in this spectacular miracle was so that when he later revealed the Eucharist, people might more readily accept him at his word. Yet despite this marvelous miracle, when Jesus ultimately puts their faith to the test, they only demand more signs as their forefathers had done before them in the desert. To drive home the sad similarity, John applies to them the same word Exodus (16:2) used of their ancestors. There we read they "grumbled" or "murmured" against Moses.

In the Bread of Life Discourse Jesus uses bread in two different and distinct senses. He begins with a symbolic sense of bread from the Old Testament. With people ever hungering to know about God and his ways, the Old Testament came to use bread as a symbol for revelation about God. In Deuteronomy (8:3) we read, "Not by bread alone does man live but by every word that comes from the mouth of the Lord." In the same vein Amos (8:11) speaks of a "famine not of bread, a drought not of water, but of hearing the word of the Lord." In the beginning of the discourse, then, Jesus speaks of himself as the bread of life in the Old Testament sense of his being and bringing God's revelation. As God's eternal Son, Jesus is the perfect manifestation of God the Father, he is the pinnacle of all revelation. If people but accept him and follow his teaching, he assures them, they will discover the way to eternal life.

The Jewish audience correctly understood bread at the opening of the discourse in the sense of revelation from heaven, as we see in their murmuring. They argue, "Is this not Jesus, the son of Joseph? Do we not know his father and mother? Then how can he say, 'I have come down from heaven'?" (6:42). They feel they know his (human) origins and so conclude incorrectly that he cannot have come down from heaven. But Jesus only reaffirms his assertion: "Amen, amen I say to you, he who believes has eternal life. I am the bread of life" (6:47).

Then in the latter part of the discourse, which we read today, Jesus changes from the Old Testament sense of bread of heaven to a deeper New Testament significance. In speaking of bread Jesus moves from a simply figurative or symbolic level to the realm of the concrete and physical. He introduces Eucharistic overtones for the first time and refers to himself as living bread come down from heaven that will give everlasting life. He next identifies this bread with his flesh which, he avows, people must eat in order to live forever. At the end of the discourse, therefore, Jesus is clearly speaking of bread as his body and blood, which he declares is real food. Though many deny the Real Presence and claim that Jesus is merely speaking figuratively here, the text does not support their view. The bystanders unquestionably took Jesus literally when they asked, "How can this man give us [his] flesh to eat?" And even more telling, Jesus did nothing to soften his stance when they turned their backs on him and began to walk away in disgust. Had he been speaking figuratively or symbolically, a simple clarification would have prevented the needless mass defection that followed.

Two reflections come to mind. (1) In the double image Jesus used for bread in the Bread of Life Discourse, we see a preview of the Mass. Jesus first spoke of himself as bread in the symbolic sense of revelation, then in the very real sense of his body and blood in the Eucharist. At Mass each day we are first nourished by the word of God in Sacred Scripture. Here we get to know God and his ways better. We are then fed with the Eucharist, the body and blood of Jesus, which is real food for the soul. The Eucharist unites us with Jesus here on earth and gives us a foretaste of heaven. (2) Jesus invites us to share in the bread of life and warns of the consequences of failing to do so. The story of Karen Carpenter serves as a sad analogy. Karen was a popular singer in the seventies. Blessed with a voice as clear as a bell, she made millions of dollars and had many top ten hit records with her brother. Yet she died tragically at the height of her career from anorexia. She, who could have comfortably afforded anything she wanted, would not eat enough simply to stay alive. Jesus offers us the gift of the Eucharist. He encourages us to participate and partake in this inestimable gift. Yet many hold back. Some refuse to believe. Others will not bestir themselves. Still others eat barely enough to survive. Let us pray for a deep devotion to the Eucharist so that we will receive it fervently and frequently all our life long.

Commitment

There is a common theme running through all three readings for today's liturgy: the importance of commitment and the continued need to reconfirm that commitment. Let's look at all three readings, saving the most contentious and controversial for last.

The first reading is from Joshua's farewell address to the people. Joshua was the great general who, as Moses' successor, finally led the Jewish people across the Jordan River into the Promised Land where he then proceeded to clear it of their enemies. Before he died he summoned the twelve tribes of Israel, reminded them of all the good God had done for them, and asked them to renew their covenant commitment to Yahweh. Mindful of the many times they had failed Yahweh during their forty-year odyssey through the desert, including the time they had sinned by idolatry when they bowed down in worship before a golden calf at the foot of Mt. Sinai while Moses was with God at the mountaintop, Joshua's dying request is that the people commit themselves henceforth to be true to their covenantal promises and prove themselves true Israelites. To this end, Joshua pledges his whole household and urges all the tribes to follow suit. Like the patriarchs before him, Joshua was acutely aware of human weakness, his own and his people's, and so before he dies he reminds the Jewish people of the continual need to renew their covenant with God.

As the background for today's Gospel, let us recall that Jesus has for the first time hinted at the beautiful but challenging concept of the Eucharist and just recently proclaimed to the bewildered crowd the need to eat his body and drink his blood. As a result, many simply turned away and lost all interest in following him. Disappointed and saddened, Jesus then turns to those closest to him and asks the twelve if they want to leave him too. As head of the Apostles, Simon Peter answers for himself and the rest, "Master, to whom shall we go? You have the words of eternal life." They are bold words of recommitment to Jesus and his mission which, though heartfelt and sincere, Jesus realizes involve more bluster than substance. Jesus knows all too well one of the twelve will betray him (Jn 6:70), the rest will turn and run, and Peter will three times publicly disown him out of fear of being recognized as his disciple (Jn 13:38).

But the point John is driving home at this crucial juncture in the ministry of Jesus and the lives of the Apostles is their need to renew and reaffirm their faith in Jesus. Their doing so is no guarantee against all future failures but without the renewal they would fall farther away from Jesus and be in an even more precarious position. History records that through such repeated renewals they eventually strengthened their faith to the point that all, save John, freely laid down their lives and died cruel martyrs' deaths for Jesus. Faced with ferocious persecutions from both the Jewish and Roman worlds, the early Christians for whom John wrote were encouraged by this Gospel segment to keep their faith strong by frequent reaffirmations of their commitment to God, Jesus, and the Church.

The second reading (Eph 5:21-32) is particularly nettlesome because it is easily misunderstood. This was the Epistle that was traditionally read at nuptial masses prior to Vatican II. Fortuitously it was read in Latin and most brides were blissfully unaware of its import. Today with the great strides made by the women's movement it often raises hackles. In this era of equality between the sexes the idea of asking a wife to be subordinate to her husband seems sinister and strangely out of sync. But to grasp Paul's intent, the whole passage should be understood in the light of the first sentence: "Be subordinate to one another out of reverence for Christ." This is the topic sentence setting the tone for the whole passage. And it is addressed to men as well as women, husbands as well as wives. All are asked to be subordinate.

In today's world being subordinate is often viewed as demeaning and degrading, little better than being a doormat, something completely unattractive, bordering on the repulsive. In our society we much prefer self-assertiveness, self-aggrandizement. But first-century Christians saw things differently. They were particularly moved by two of Jesus' sayings which the old lectionary translated roughly as: "I have not come to be served but to serve" (Mk 10:45) and "The greatest among you is the one who serves the needs of all" (Lk 22:26). To this day the Pope still signs his letters, "The servant of the servants of God." In imitation of Jesus the early Church was even willing to carry service over into sacrifice, recalling Jesus' challenge to the Christian, "Greater love than this no one has than to lay down his life for his friend" (Jn 15:13).

Still, on the surface, the heaviest burden in today's Epistle seems to fall on the woman. She is asked to submit, to obey—one almost gets the sense of kowtowing—while the husband is simply asked to love his wife. Some today may think of love in terms of love letters and flowers but Paul has something decidedly differ-ent in mind. He asks the man to love his wife as Christ loved the Church. And how did Christ love the Church, i.e., the people of God? We need only glance at a crucifix. Jesus loved us so much he gave his life to save us from eternal damnation. Thus the love Paul asks of a husband for his wife, is a love so deep the husband would freely lay down his life for her. In short, Paul challenges both husband and wife to strive to outdo each other in showing that selfless love one for the other that Jesus did for us.

All three readings for today are as challenging as they are beautiful. They invite us to renew our commitment and covenant love with God our Father and to show forth that love in our care and concern for others. Yet commitment is something the modern world often finds difficult. Lifelong commitment and fidelity, as in Christian marriage, many modern men and women think of as humanly impossible. But nothing is impossible for God, and our forebears by and large did much better than we in this regard. Let us pray, therefore, for all people today that we be ever true to God and to each other.

Laws of Ritual Purification

In today's Gospel the Pharisees complain to Jesus that his disciples fail to observe the laws of ritual purification. Jewish law at the time consisted of two components: the Torah and the Talmud, Scripture and oral tradition. Of the two, the Torah was the more important and sacred. It consisted of the first five books of the Old Testament which were generally attributed to Moses himself. In the Torah there are 613 precepts, including the Ten Commandments, which were regarded as divinely inspired. Since many of these precepts were general in nature and the human heart craves specifics, rabbinical interpretations of the law developed over time to flesh out the commands and make them more concrete. These humanly conceived accretions to the law became part of an oral tradition that numbered thousands of additional prescriptions that were later codified in the Talmud and regarded as equally binding by the Pharisees.

The rules of ritual purification mentioned in today's Gospel were part of the oral or Talmudic tradition. Tracing their evolution affords some insight into the Pharisaic mindset. Scripture scholars surmise these particular rules sprang from a desire to replicate in ordinary society the ritual holiness of the priesthood and Temple. Priests were expected to wash before approaching Yahweh or the altar (Ex 40:30-33). In emulation of the priests, therefore, oral tradition called for the people to wash before praying. All offerings presented to the Temple were routinely sprinkled to purify them. The Talmud subsequently posited food from the market be similarly sprinkled. Priests had to be clean to partake of the communion sacrifice (Lv 7:20). Since all food is a gift of God, the Jewish people were likewise enjoined to wash their hands before eating. Thus, over time even the laity were saddled with ceremonial obligations similar in nature to those designed for the select and privileged priesthood. Herein lies the core of a major complaint Jesus had against the Pharisees who unfortunately dominated Jewish religious thinking at the time. The Pharisees strove for the ideal themselves but then ended up imposing it on others as the norm.

Though pious and well intended, the many man-made accretions to the law created insuperable problems for ordinary people who lived in an arid land where water was not readily accessible. What little water was available to them had always to be carried home, one jug at a time, usually perched on the head of the woman of the house. Peasants working in fields far from home, for instance, often had no water to wash the food they picked for their lunch. To eat it unsprinkled was to break the law; observing the law meant they had to go hungry. A merchant in the market who might want to pray during a lull in sales but with no nearby source of water to perform the prior ablutions could not do so without violating the law. Instead of bringing people closer to God, the Talmudic laws of ritual purification ended up an insurmountable obstacle. As a result, people felt the need for further distinctions. They distinguished between the full oral tradition called the "Great Tradition," which only people of means living within city limits could hope to observe, and the "Little Tradition," a practical adaptation scaled down to reflect peasant realities and country conditions.

The Pharisees placed little stock in this latter distinction as seen in today's Gospel where they criticize the Apostles for not fulfilling the Great Tradition. Their carping continues an ongoing conflict between them and Jesus and sparks further controversy. In response to their challenge, Jesus alludes to the distinction between the Torah and the Talmud, the first divinely inspired, the second humanly contrived, and quotes from Isaiah (29:13), "This people honors me with their lips, but their hearts are far from me; in vain do they worship me, teaching as doctrines mere human precepts." The Pharisaic preoccupation with outward appearances and their fixation on externals, such as is manifested in their insistence on the purification of the surfaces of such things as cups, jugs, and kettles, threaten the basic thrust of the Law which is towards love of God and love of neighbor. Such love calls for radical inner conversion and purging. Cleansing cups and washing pots and hands can all be done without interior realignment or transformation, without any sign or act of love, and so have no real intrinsic connection to true religion.

In opposition to the Pharisees' emphasis on externals, Jesus boldly declares the only thing that can make a person unclean is what comes from within, from the heart. He then illustrates what he means with a list of sins that offend both God and humankind: murder, theft, adultery, deceit. His concluding example, an obtuse spirit, is a thinly veiled barb at the Pharisees. Jesus had only recently multiplied the loaves and fish that fed over 5000 people (Mk 6:34-44), something that could not have escaped the attention of the ever curious, constantly inquisitive Pharisees. Yet they gave him no sign of recognition and still refused to acknowledge that his power came from God. In remaining wedded to their inane presupposition that his power came from Beelzebul (Mk 3:22), their behavior represented a classic case of an obtuse spirit.

The responsorial psalm for today also mirrors Jesus' attitude toward religion. The first line (15:1), unfortunately omitted, asks, "Lord, who may abide in your tent? Who may dwell on your holy mountain?" In reply the psalmist spells out what one must do to be close to God. Notice all the psalmist's recommendations reflect an inner conversion from self-centeredness to love of God and neighbor that Jesus has consistently called for: to walk blamelessly, do justice, think the truth, slander not, harm not, reproach not, lend not at usury, accept no bribe.

Cure of the Deaf Mute

The passage we read from Isaiah today was moved forward in the text by the original compilers of the manuscript in order to round out the first part of the book, which is generally attributed to First Isaiah. This particular composition, however, is more likely the work of Second Isaiah who labored among the exiles in Babylon to keep their faith alive. The poetic vision he proffers of a time in which the eyes of the blind would be opened, the ears of the deaf cleared, the lame would leap like a stag, and the tongues of the dumb would sing, was intended to bolster the exiles' hope of eventual return to Jerusalem and restoration of their nation. Speaking figuratively, through a series of powerful metaphors, he compares the elation the exiles will experience on returning home to the thrill of a blind man seeing for the first time, a deaf person hearing her first sound, a cripple at long last able to move freely about, a mute first calling a loved one by name. Centuries later, long after their return to the Holy Land, the Jews believed similar signs would signal the coming of the Messiah.

To help his readers recognize the Old Testament allusion and understand the curing of the deaf-mute both as a fulfillment of Isaiah's prophecy and an unmistakable sign of the beginning of messianic times, Mark uses the very same word for mute that the Greek translation of Isaiah used, *mogilalos*, a highly unusual word found nowhere else in Scripture. Throughout his Gospel Mark likewise continues to show that what Isaiah foretold and dreamed of figuratively, Jesus fulfilled literally. Here Jesus restores the man's hearing and speech. Earlier he cured a paralytic in Capernaum and sent him on his way home (Mk 2:1-12). Later he will restore a blind beggar's sight at Bethsaida (Mk 8:22-26).

With illness popularly perceived as evidence of Satan's control, each miracle also provided added evidence that the kingdom

153

of God was breaking forth upon the earth in the presence of Jesus. Moreover, each miracle had a spiritual dimension and purpose. Jesus restored the physically blind to sight so those spiritually blind might more easily recognize him as God's Son. He opened the ears of the deaf so those who closed their ears to his word might offer him a fairer hearing. He helped the lame to walk so people would not fear to follow him. What Isaiah could only dream of in Old Testament times, Jesus brought to fulfillment in New Testament times.

Deafness in ancient times, as now, is a terrible handicap. People who cannot hear generally find it hard to speak because they cannot imitate sounds. Unable to hear or speak, they are cut off from basic communication and ordinary conversation which help to form personalities and friendships. Though often mistaken as dimwitted and dull as a result, their inability to communicate is simply another dreadful consequence of their unfortunate physical disability. Helen Keller who achieved remarkable success despite being both blind and deaf from a tragic childhood illness always maintained deafness was a far more debilitating and oppressive handicap than blindness.

Though Helen learned to speak with the help of a bright and indefatigable tutor, Annie Sullivan, most people born deaf in ancient times were doomed to be mute as well. Worse, muteness was commonly regarded as a stigma, a sign of God's displeasure. When the people offended God by their distance or disobedience, the prophetic voice often grew silent. It generally did not return until the people repented or begged God to break the silence. Muteness was likewise associated with a lack of faith. Recall how Zechariah was struck dumb for refusing to believe the angel who announced the birth of his son, John the Baptist. Not surprisingly, then, the cure of the deaf-mute is intimately connected with faith. It was performed in response to his faith and the faith of the people who brought him to Jesus. It was also intended to lead others to faith. A mute gaining the power of speech was a sure sign of God at work in Jesus and highly likely to influence others toward faith.

Another important facet of the story is the deaf-mute is a Gentile or non-Jew living in a Gentile area. Jesus takes him apart from the crowd to cure him because the crowd at large does not have faith. And in the absence of faith Jesus often found it difficult to work cures or perform miracles (Mk 6:5-6). Some see the deaf-mute as the male counterpart of the Syrophoenician woman whose daughter Jesus had cured of an evil spirit immediately prior to this miracle (Mk 7:24-30). Both were Gentiles, both had faith strong enough to elicit cures from Jesus, and both remained behind in pagan territory to bear witness to Jesus and what he had miraculously done for them. This provides a hint of universalism early in Mark's Gospel, suggesting the Good News of God's love for humankind was to be shared with Gentiles and not limited to Jews alone. It showed Gentiles were also capable of hearing God's call and of being instrumental in attracting others.

The early Church was evidently much moved by this Gospel narrative. They saw the curing of the deaf-mute as symbolic of what happens spiritually to all Christians when they open themselves up to God and accept Jesus in their lives. God first opens our ears to receive his word into our hearts and then expects us to proclaim the good news of salvation to others. Not surprisingly, this passage quickly became part of the Church's baptismal ceremony and message. Even in today's sacrament of Baptism the priest touches the ears and mouth of the one to be baptized and prays that they be opened to God's word, using the very same command Jesus used in today's Gospel, "Ephphatha!" As a result, Christians see in their baptismal vows the obligation always to be attentive to the word of God in their lives and ever ready to proclaim it to others in all they say and do.

"You Are the Messiah"

In Chapter 8 of his Gospel from which we read today Mark begins to focus on the passion and death of Jesus. In each of the three chapters immediately preceding Jesus' entrance into Jerusalem (Mk 11:1), Mark records one of the three occasions in which Jesus predicts his passion, death, and resurrection (8:31, 9:31, 10:33-34), followed up immediately by a lesson in discipleship (8:34-38, 9:33-37, 10:35-45). To understand the interchange between Jesus and the Apostles in today's first prediction of the passion, we should examine it in the context of the cure of the blind man which immediately preceded it (8:22-26), but which regrettably is not included in the Sunday lectionary readings.

In that cure at Bethsaida Jesus takes the blind man aside, rubs his eyes with spittle (which in Old Testament times was thought to have curative powers), and asks if he can see. The man replies he can see, but only vaguely; people look like trees walking around. Jesus then lays hands on him and he is at last able to see clearly. Part of the reason for drawing the miracle out in stages is to give the man and all who witness his cure more time to recognize the power of God as it works through Jesus. This miracle, like all the others, was intended to help people understand who Jesus really was and thus help them come to believe in him.

Fresh from having helped the blind man to see physically, Jesus next tries to help his disciples to see with the eyes of faith so they might better understand who he truly is. He asks them who people say he is, but he is clearly more interested in what they themselves think. They simply reiterate the views commonly held by the crowds: John the Baptist, Elijah, one of the prophets of old. Despite their three years of close association with Jesus, it is clear they still have no inkling, no clue, of who Jesus really is.

Only Peter has caught a glimmer of who Jesus might be. With

typical brashness he declares Jesus is the Christ, which means the Messiah. "Messiah" literally means "the anointed," and "Christ" is simply a shortened form of the Greek word for "anointed." This declaration of Peter's marks the high point of the first half of Mark's Gospel. Mark began his Gospel by identifying Jesus as the Christ in his very first sentence (1:1) but no one in the Gospel narrative has come close to recognizing it or accepting it until Peter at this moment. The crowds have often expressed amazement at what Jesus has been able to accomplish in terms of his many healings and miracles. The people have openly pondered where his power came from and what manner of man he might be. But no one up until now has drawn the correct conclusion. In Matthew's account of the same story (Mt 16:13-20), Jesus is so impressed by Peter's profession of faith that he invests Peter on the spot with primacy in the Church.

The setting of today's Gospel at Caesarea Philippi also makes Peter's profession of faith all the more powerful and significant. Caesarea Philippi was home to Herod Philip, son of Herod the Great. Herod Philip had expanded the city and added his own name to it to distinguish it from the larger and more important coastal city of Caesarea, which had been built by his father and included a huge man-made harbor that afforded Israel its only deep-water access to the Mediterranean Sea. Herod the Great had earlier constructed a temple in Caesarea Philippi to honor the then reigning Roman emperor, Augustus Caesar, who in his lifetime declared himself a god and demanded his subjects worship him. To this city citizens and subjects of Rome were compelled to come each year to perform their annual obligatory adoration of the divine Augustus. Ironically, it is in this pagan city under the shadow of the temple of this self-deified Roman emperor that Peter boldly declares Jesus is the Messiah, God's anointed or chosen one.

The joy of the moment was not unalloyed, however. Like the blind man in the preceding incident, Peter does not yet see distinctly. So Jesus makes use of Peter's unusually strong declaration of faith to reveal more about himself and God's ultimate plan for him. He forewarns his disciples for the very first time of his upcoming passion, death, and resurrection. Resurrection was something they could not even conceive of until well after Jesus had risen from the dead. But they knew what suffering and death meant and it terrified them. More importantly, it was not what they or any of their contemporaries expected for the Messiah. Most people at the time gave short shrift to the Suffering Servant Songs of Isaiah (Is 40-55), part of which comprises today's first reading. They concentrated instead on the Son of Man theme in the Book of Daniel. The Son of Man was expected to receive power and dominion over all the nations (Dn 7:13-14).

Frequently, human action turns on very mixed motivation. Partly out of genuine concern for Jesus' welfare, partly from a selfish craving to share in the spoils of a successful sovereign, and partly from an honest desire to set Jesus straight on the true nature of the Messiah as he and popular opinion understood it, Peter tries in vain to dissociate Jesus from the concept of a suffering Messiah. As a result, Peter faces the full fury of Jesus' justifiable rage. Jesus brands him a Satan for contradicting God's plans and trying to dissuade the Lord's anointed from surrendering to God's will. From a position of the highest possible prior praise, Peter is brought very low indeed.

After this first prediction of the passion, as with the next two, Jesus immediately goes on to clarify the nature of a true disciple. Anyone wishing to follow him, he warns, will likewise have to bear a cross. It is a stern message that strikes fear in the hearts of most of us. Yet suffering and sorrow are part of all life. Jesus does not promise to deliver us from difficulties. He merely promises to help us in our struggles. Moreover, his resurrection from the dead assures us that the rewards of eternal life, which are beyond imagining, will be ours if we remain faithful to God's will.

Second Prediction of the Passion

In this section of Mark's Gospel Jesus three times predicts his passion, death, and resurrection. In last week's Gospel Jesus for the first time warned the Apostles that he must suffer, die, and rise from the dead. Resurrection was a concept they could not even begin to fathom. When Jesus openly refers to it again shortly afterwards, immediately following the Transfiguration, they ponder among themselves what resurrection could mean (Mk 9:10). Jesus then performs a miracle to help them better understand the concept of resurrection (9:14-29).

A man from the crowd calls out to Jesus asking him to cure his son who is an epileptic demoniac. The boy has long been possessed by a demon who over the years has rendered him mute, subjected him to convulsions, and attempted to destroy him by throwing him into fire and water. Jesus commands the unclean spirit to leave the child and immediately it does, leaving its erstwhile victim lying lifeless, like a corpse, on the ground. Bystanders are convinced he is dead, but Jesus takes him by the hand and helps him to his feet. In showing mastery over Satan who brought sickness and death into the world, Jesus is demonstrating to his disciples that he has not only the power to heal the body but also to restore it to life. Earlier in Mark's Gospel Jesus had raised the daughter of Jairus to life (Mk 5:21-43) and other evangelists report he raised the son of the widow of Nain (Lk 7:11-17) and Lazarus, the brother of Martha and Mary (Jn 11:1-44).

Having afforded the Apostles ample reason to accept the veracity and efficacy of his word, Jesus proceeds to predict his passion, death, and resurrection for the second time. This time he carefully hones his phrasing to specify he will be "handed over" or "delivered" into the hands of evil men, selecting a word that in both the Old and New Testaments was frequently linked to the fate of prophets and God's faithful. But once again the Apostles fail to grasp Jesus' message. Still they dare not question him further. Subconsciously they don't want to think of suffering and hence have no desire for Jesus to expand on the topic. Consciously they are still reeling from Jesus' stinging rebuke of Peter consequent upon Jesus' first prediction of the passion.

In Mark's Gospel each of the three predictions of the passion is followed by a lesson in discipleship. After the first prediction Jesus told his disciples of the need for them likewise to take up their cross each day and follow him. After this, the second prediction, Jesus introduces the discipleship lesson with a question. His Apostles' response makes painfully clear how little they understood of his teaching despite close daily contact and near constant instruction over three years. Jesus simply asks what they were discussing as they walked along the road but the Apostles balk at replying. They remain shamefacedly silent because Jesus has caught them arguing over perks and pecking orders, privileges and priorities. Unlike Simon's mother-in-law who had earlier demonstrated the true nature of discipleship by getting up immediately upon her cure and waiting on Jesus and the disciples (Mk 1:31), the Apostles are still centered on self, preoccupied with personal enrichment and advancement. Even later in the Gospel when the other Apostles criticize James and John for their crassness in seeking the highest places in Jesus' kingdom (Mk 10:41), it is patently obvious their only regret is they had not been churlish enough to beat the two brothers to the punch.

To counter this dangerous drift away from all he wanted to inculcate in his followers, Jesus begins to teach his Apostles anew. He deliberately sits down because being seated was a position of authority in ancient times. Rabbis sat to make formal pronouncements, much as judges today give their rulings while seated at the bench. It is a seemingly small detail that can easily escape modern notice but to the Jewish contemporaries of Jesus it was an unmistakable sign Jesus was about to give an important teaching.

Jesus begins by reversing the prevailing order in society at the time in which the influential dominated the weak. In his kingdom he tells us the highest ranking is reserved for the one who is the servant of all (Mk 9:35). For servant Jesus uses the word *diakonos* from which our word "deacon" is derived. But while the role of deacon may be esteemed in the modern Church, in pre-Christian times it decidedly was not. A deacon ranked only slightly higher than a slave, and the most disagreeable, distasteful, and dangerous jobs were routinely reserved for them. After this deliberately shocking image and still another prediction of the passion (Mk 10:32-34), Jesus ultimately concludes by asking us to imitate him who "did not come to be served but to serve and to give his life as a ransom for the many" (Mk 10:45). In short, Jesus asks the same selfless love in the service of others that led him to offer his life on the cross.

The second image of a child which Jesus uses in today's Gospel is equally startling. In Mark Jesus urges us to *receive* a child (Mk 9:37); in Matthew Jesus adds we should *humble ourselves* like a child (Mt 18:4). To understand the import of Mark's image, recall a child is born helpless and cannot survive without nurturing and protection. In selecting this image, then, Jesus commands us to care for those who are least able to provide for themselves, much as God the Father freely takes care of all our needs. To comprehend Matthew's image, remember that in the ancient Middle East, as in many less developed countries today and even among migrant workers within our own borders, children were rarely pampered. They generally had to work full days with their parents in the fields just so the family could survive. The subservient role of children in the Middle East was even reflected in language. In Aramaic, for instance, the common language spoken in Palestine at the time of Jesus, the word for child is exactly the same as the word for servant: *talya*. Matthew's presentation of Jesus' call to humble ourselves like little children, then, is simply another call to service, reinforcing the notion that in imitation of Jesus we are to die to selfishness and sin and devote ourselves as completely as possible to the service of others.

In this day and age when abortion is not only permitted but promoted in our own country and many other parts of the world, Jesus' words, "whoever welcomes a child welcomes me," are a strong indication of where Christians should stand. They reveal Jesus' perception of the proper Christian attitude with regard to children and the underprivileged. His words say volumes of the vital role of parents who lovingly accept children in God's name and spend their lives loving them and caring for them and of individuals who fight to help and support the needy and afflicted. His words also say volumes of those couples and individuals who open their hearts and homes to children in adoption and thus freely commit themselves to a lifetime of love and service of God's most helpless angels.

"Whoever Is Not Against Us Is for Us"

In today's Gospel and in Luke 9:50 Jesus tells us that anyone who is not against him is for him. In Luke 11:23 and Matthew 12:30, however, he says just the opposite. There he says anyone who is not for him is against him. People often find the apparent contradiction confusing and disturbing. Similar incidents occur in the Old Testament. In Isaiah 2:4 and later in Micah 4:3, Yahweh orders his people to hammer their swords into plowshares, their spears into sickles. But in Joel 4:10 God adopts the contrary position and tells them to hammer their plowshares into swords, their pruning hooks into spears. While fundamentalists hold Scripture must be taken literally, the juxtaposition of these seemingly contradictory statements clearly illustrates the need to interpret Scripture in context. As you recall from the temptation of Jesus in the desert, even the devil can quote Scripture for his own ends (Mt 4:6).

Large bodies of literature frequently contain contradictions. Take the treasury of English maxims we pass on from generation to generation. We say, "Look before you leap." But we also say, "He who hesitates is lost." A direct contradiction! We say, "Many hands make the work light." But we also say, "Too many cooks spoil the broth." Yet these contradictions don't bother or disturb us. We know that while contradictory on the surface, each is apposite in appropriate circumstances. So it is with the Bible. We have to take things in context. Apparent contradictions are usually due to strikingly different circumstances, as we shall see.

In Jesus' first statement, anyone not against me is for me, Jesus is responding to a complaint by the Apostles. They have discovered a stranger expelling demons in his name. Since he is not one of their number and thus not officially missioned by Jesus, the Apostles order him to stop. When they report this to Jesus, he promptly disagrees with their decision and tries to dissuade them from doing so again. He assures them that anyone who invokes his name to seek God's help in curing others cannot be working against him. The name of Jesus is no magic mantra that cures independently of the one so named. For a cure to be successful the person must have faith in the power of Jesus to effectuate the cure. And since that power is reserved ultimately to God alone, anyone succeeding in a cure through Jesus' name must in fact accept Jesus' unique relationship to God. Given the circumstances of the man's invoking Jesus' name and the happy outcome that ensues, Jesus deduces the man must have faith and be on their side.

The second statement from Luke 11:23, in which Jesus says he who is not for me is against me, by way of contrast, is addressed to people who immediately before adamantly refused to believe Jesus was from God. Jesus had just performed a riveting miracle by driving a demon from a mute and enabling him to speak. While those with an open mind reacted favorably and stood in awe of Jesus and what he had accomplished, a disgruntled faction, which Matthew 12:24 identifies as Pharisees and Mark 3:22 classifies as scribes, farcically complains that Jesus performs his miracles through the power of Beelzebul. Since it is clear that the members of this group have closed their minds and hearts to him, Jesus is forced to conclude they are not with him but against him. So the two statements, while seemingly contradictory, simply reflect Jesus' reaction to two completely different situations. It is only when taken out of context that they are misleading.

The two statements from the Old Testament are likewise in response to widely differing circumstances. Isaiah 2:4 speaks of a time when God will establish his kingdom. In this messianic era there will be no conflict, no war, no need for swords or spears. The call to abandon arms also dovetails perfectly with First Isaiah's overall message. First Isaiah wrote at a time when the people were looking to military might and foreign political alliances to preserve their independence (cf. Third Sunday of Advent B). He was sent precisely to warn the people against such folly and to redirect them back to God. If the Jewish people would simply trust in God and follow his ways, he assured them, Yahweh would protect them and they would have no further need of arms. Joel 4:10, on the other hand, is offering an apocalyptic vision of what will take place at the end of time when Yahweh comes to settle accounts with the wayward nations that have abused Israel. On that terrible Day of the Lord when wrongs would be redressed and earlier misdeeds punished, swords and spears would indeed be needed to execute Yahweh's judgment against the offending nations.

Today's Gospel also demonstrates another reason for the need of interpretation in Scripture. Jesus speaks of cutting off one's hands and feet. In doing so he is using Semitic exaggeration or what today we call hyperbole. Jesus is simply exaggerating to emphasize his point. He in no way intends to be taken literally. It's akin to someone today saying he'd give his right arm to see the World Series. To expect his arm in payment would be an absurd and grotesque misreading.

Ancient Hebrew was also in many ways a poetic language which frequently used symbols to convey abstract ideas. Hands and feet, for example, were natural symbols for purposeful activity. In effect Jesus is saying that if the activity we perform with our hands or feet offends God, we should stop the activity. Similarly, the eye is the opening to the mind. The image Jesus uses here simply suggests that if we have evil thoughts, we must redirect our focus. In short, if we would go to great length to avoid the loss of an arm, leg, or eye, how much more should we be willing to do to avoid the loss of our immortal souls?

The Question of Divorce

The setting for today's Gospel is Judea, in an area on the far side of the Jordan, also known as Perea. Mark begins the passage by telling us the Pharisees approached Jesus to test him in the sense of trapping him. They cunningly ask about divorce while Jesus is in the territory of Herod Antipas, son of Herod the Great, who only recently had beheaded John the Baptist for speaking out against his unlawful and adulterous relationship with Herodias, his brother Philip's wife (Mk 6:17-29). The Pharisees were no doubt hoping Jesus would likewise stir Herod's ire with his reply and end up suffering a fate similar to John's.

Jesus responds by asking what Moses taught on the matter. The Pharisees reply correctly that Moses permitted divorce and a decree of divorce. They refer to Deuteronomy (24:1-4) which says a man may divorce his wife by writing out a decree of divorce and handing it to her if he finds her guilty of "some impropriety" or "something indecent." The vagueness of the term which provided the grounds for divorce offered a field day to subsequent generations of rabbis. Conservative rabbis, in the tradition of Shammai, held only a grievous breach of the marriage vows, such as adultery, was sufficient grounds for divorce. Liberal rabbis from the school of Hillel, however, gradually whittled away at the norm over time until it became meaningless. It eventually came to encompass anything and everything that could possibly cause the husband displeasure, including burning his toast or putting too much starch in his tunic.

Jesus counters their argument by pointing out Moses granted the dispensation because of their hardness of heart. By this he means Moses did not permit divorce in the sense of approving it, promoting it, or encouraging it. He merely acknowledged it as a fact of life that human intransigence would not yield on. Up to the time of Moses divorce was in fact commonplace. A man could divorce his wife at any time, for any reason. A woman, on the other hand, could leave her husband but never divorce him. This was manifestly unfair to the woman. Since a man had the power to divorce his wife at will, he could remarry at any time. A woman, however, needed proof of divorce to contract a second marriage, something a vindictive husband could easily withhold. And a woman in ancient times without a man to provide for her and protect her was in a pitiable state, as the story of Naomi in the Book of Ruth plaintively attests. Hence Moses' enjoinder of "something indecent" as a prerequisite for divorce was intended to rein in men's unbridled freedom, help curtail the practice of divorce, and protect women from the capricious decisions of their husbands. Moses' stipulation for a written decree of divorce, called a *get*, was also aimed at leveling the playing field by providing women with the proof of divorce they needed to be legally free to remarry.

Jesus, who came to fulfill the Mosaic Law, moves to a higher plane than Moses ever dreamed possible. He proposes an ideal for marriage that was part of God's plan from the very beginning of creation. He refers to Genesis (2:18-24), our first reading, where God creates man and then seeks a suitable partner for him. God next creates all the animals of the land and all the birds of the sky but can find among them no suitable partner for man. So God fashions woman (*ishsha*) from "her man" (*isha*). From this simple but profound primordial story which tells of God purposefully creating woman to be the complement and companion of man, Jesus suggests matrimony is intended to bring to fulfillment the union between the sexes that God fashioned into them from the very beginning of creation. It is unquestionably a lofty ideal, a challenge to the very best in humankind, and an invitation to both husband and wife to manifest in their lives the love that Jesus has shown for us, the Church.

A modern translation of a Talmudic poem, written centuries before the first stirrings of the women's liberation movement, aptly sums up the creation story and God's plan for marriage. A modern day translation would read something like this. God did not create woman from man's head so that he might boss her around. God did not create woman from man's feet so that he could kick her around. God created woman from man's side so that she would always be close to his heart.

Yet lofty and admirable as it is, Jesus' vision of marriage is often difficult to achieve. We all know of many wonderful couples who tried their hand at marriage and couldn't make a go of it. We also know of individuals who entered marriage and never got a fair deal or half a chance from their partners. We even know of some who have ended up abused. The Church also recognizes the myriad problems and has tried to reach out to help the people involved in such relationships by making marriage tribunals available with the power to grant annulments.

Annulments are frequently misunderstood. To understand what an annulment is we need to know what a Christian marriage is. A Christian marriage is an irrevocable contract among three people: a man, a woman, and God. The couple promises fidelity for life and God blesses them with a sacrament. For such a marriage there must be fully informed knowledge and perfectly free consent. If one or the other is missing in at least one of the parties, the marriage may be annulled. Reasons vary but may include immaturity, psychological difficulties, substance dependence or abuse. An annulment means at least one party at the time of the marriage was incapable of entering into an irrevocable contract. It does not mean that there was no marriage or that the children are illegitimate. Since the priest is authorized by the state to officiate at weddings, every Church wedding is a legal civil marriage and the children are legitimate in both the eyes of the Church and the state. In granting an annulment the Church simply declares that at the time of the wedding the necessary preconditions for forming an irrevocable contract were not present. In the absence of an irrevocable contract, the union may be dissolved and the parties are then free to remarry.

The Rich Young Man

Today's Gospel continues to develop the theme set out at the end of last week's Gospel, "Whoever does not accept the kingdom of God like a child will not enter it" (Mk 10:15). The rich young man comes up to Jesus and asks what he must do to share in everlasting life. His use of the title, "good teacher," and his preoccupation with the deeds he must do smacks of Pharisaism. This initially seems to set Jesus on edge and immediately puts him on his guard. Jesus responds at first, therefore, by merely summarizing the commandments and making it clear the young man must keep them. When the young man replies he has observed all the commandments since childhood, Jesus realizes he is sincere and is deeply moved. He cannot help but love him and invites the young man to become his disciple.

As a precondition, however, Jesus warns the young man he must rid himself of his possessions in order to be able to follow him unencumbered. "At that statement," the story continues, "his face fell, and he went away sad, for he had many possessions" (Mk 10:22). It is one of the saddest lines in all the Gospels. The young man had been offered the chance of a lifetime, the opportunity to be close to Jesus and to share in his ministry, but he preferred the passing things of this world instead. It is the only personal invitation we see Jesus offer in the Gospels that is refused.

Jesus is also saddened by the rejection. His manifest disappointment reflects the fact that God expects more of us than merely keeping the commandments. Being a Christian involves a loving, giving, self-sacrificing relationship between the individual and God, a love modeled on the love Jesus showed for God his Father. Jesus also taught us to call God our Father. Do we expect a parent to be happy with a child who merely keeps the rules: coming home on time, cleaning up his/her room, doing well in school, taking out the garbage? These may be the rules that are necessary to survive in an intergenerational household, but they are hardly all that parents hope for or expect from a child. At a minimum, they expect love, a love that shows itself in the child's wanting to share in the life of the parents, to be like them to some extent, and hopefully to incorporate the deepest values of the parents concerning God, life, and others. So, today's Gospel suggests, it is with God. God wants us to love him freely and fully, not merely by keeping the commandments, but by emulating his Son and adopting his attitudes and ways. For God and the establishment of his kingdom, Jesus willingly surrendered all. He held nothing back, not even his life. Jesus also clearly expects his faithful followers to put God first in their lives and hold nothing back.

At the same time, however, we should note that the rich young man committed no sin by refusing to part with his many possessions and not following Jesus more closely. God desires a close, personal relationship with each of us but never demands or forces it. As a bare bone minimum, he requires no more in fact than we keep the commandments. Furthermore, wealth in itself is not evil. If it were, Jesus would have directed the young man to destroy his possessions, not give them to others who would in turn be corrupted. Jesus' injunction to give the proceeds to the poor points to a proper use of wealth that may suggest the man was less than generous with his money and unconcerned over the needs of those less fortunate than himself. His preoccupation with possessions had already robbed him of the freedom to be available to Jesus' call and deprived him of the priceless opportunity of drawing closer to Jesus and of being of service in God's kingdom. Jesus knew such a deep-rooted attachment to material things, if left unchecked, could eventually lead him away from God and toward sin, prompting Jesus to lament how hard it is for the rich to enter the kingdom of God.

The disciples were stunned by this pronouncement since riches in the Old Testament were regarded as a sure sign of divine approbation. Hence their complete bewilderment. So Jesus repeats it again, the second time comparing the chances of the rich getting into heaven to the likelihood of a camel passing through the eye of a needle. Since this is clearly impossible, many commentators have tried to explain it away. Some refer to the needle's eye as a small narrow gate next to the large city gate that could be left open when the main gate had to be closed for security purposes at times of approaching danger. A camel could conceivably fit through such a gate, though with considerable difficulty. The problem with this argument, however, is that there is no evidence such a gate in fact existed in Jerusalem. Others fasten on a few manuscripts that record "rope" (*kamilon*) instead of "camel" (*kamelon*), arguing that a thin rope could possibly pass through the eye of a very large needle. But the best scholarship seems to side with "camel" over "rope" and suggests a simple transmission error on the part of a scribe from *e* to *i* in the original Greek is responsible for "rope" in a few of the ancient manuscripts.

The soundest explanation of all, however, is that Jesus was simply using Semitic exaggeration or hyperbole. A similar example involving an elephant is found in the Talmud. Jesus, in brief, was deliberately overstating his case to drive home his point. In doing so he shocked the Apostles to full attention and forced them to ask the right question: Then who can be saved? Their dismay reflects the common Jewish belief that God rewards the good in this life with material prosperity and withholds it from the evil (Dt 28:1-14). The Pharisees pushed this faulty premise to the limit and concluded individuals could therefore earn heaven on the basis of their own accomplishments. Jesus' overriding purpose in this entire section, therefore, is to correct this erroneous view and set the record straight. Salvation originates from God, and not from humankind. It is God who saves us in his gracious free will, not we who earn or merit heaven by dint of our efforts or good deeds. God wants and indeed requires our cooperation in working out our salvation, but it is always he who initiates the process and sustains us in its unfolding. Salvation is from God!

Not To Be Served, But To Serve

All four Gospels record that Jesus three times predicted his passion, death, and resurrection. In Mark all three predictions are met with an abysmal lack of sensitivity and understanding on the part of the Apostles that compels Jesus to reinforce and redefine precisely what the true nature and responsibility of discipleship entails. Today's Gospel segment reveals the serious misconceptions that still prevailed after the third and final prediction of the passion. The incident unfortunately speaks volumes of the Apostles' tenuous state of preparedness for their apostolate and mission at the time.

After the first prediction of the passion (Mk 8:31), Peter tried to convince Jesus otherwise. But Jesus would not be dissuaded and insisted even his disciples had to take up their cross. After the second prediction of the passion (9:31), Jesus caught the Apostles shamelessly arguing among themselves as to who was the greatest. He promptly set a child in their midst as a model of discipleship and told them they must become like little children if they were ever to find a place in the kingdom of God. In today's Gospel, immediately on the heels on the third prediction (10:33-34), James and John approach Jesus and, seemingly oblivious of what he has just said of himself and all he has previously tried to teach them, presumptuously ask to sit at either side of him in his glory. In ancient times sitting immediately next to the king translated into the highest position of honor at court and the pinnacle of power in government. In essence, the two brothers were seeking to become the most important and powerful people in Jesus' kingdom. Stunned and saddened by their brash request, Jesus simply asks whether they can drink of the cup he will drink from and be baptized in the same bath of pain. Both images are steeped in biblical significance.

In ancient times the father of the family apportioned the food and wine for each member of his family. They were expected to eat and drink whatever he set before them. The cup eventually came to symbolize one's portion or fate in life, particularly as assigned by God in his role as Father. We see it in Isaiah when he tells the exiles in their anguish that they have drunk the cup of Yahweh's wrath (51:17) and again in Psalm 16:5 which describes Yahweh as "my allotted portion and my cup" in the sense of destiny or fate. Jesus also uses the image later when in Gethsemane he prays to his Father, "Take this cup away from me" (Mk 14:36). Here Jesus uses the cup image to underscore his role as a suffering Messiah and to ask James and John if they are prepared to share in the suffering God will shortly ask of him.

The word "baptized" or "immersed," as used here, has none of the Christian connotations of baptism. It is used in the figurative sense of submerged or overwhelmed in difficulty or emotion, such as a debtor sunk in debt or a widow mired in grief. In like vein, the psalmist describes his sorrow in terms of Yahweh's waves and breakers rolling over him (Ps 42:8) and Israel's later escape from sure destruction in terms of the waters that would have closed over them, the torrent that would have swept them away (Ps 124:4). Jesus uses the image to warn once again of the danger and hardship that will lie ahead for all who follow him.

Nevertheless the other Apostles still pay little heed. Mark simply reports they were indignant at the churlish behavior of their two companions, both of whom had been singled out together with Peter for special attention and mentoring by Jesus (Mk 9:2). But one suspects the real reason for their pique was that these sons of Zebedee had been quicker off the mark in trying to corner the perks and privileges of the kingdom they all still expected to be glorious. Hence Jesus tries for the third time to disabuse them of their foolish fantasies. He purposely pits the prevailing pagan power structure against the appropriate disposition he would like to see in his disciples. Among the Gentiles important people did as they wished with impunity. At his inauguration as Roman Emperor, Galba blithely boasted that he was now free to do whatever he wanted to whomever he wanted. In sharp contrast Jesus turns this sad world order upside down by proclaiming those considered great in his kingdom will be those who serve the needs of all.

Jesus then concludes his teaching on discipleship with a single sentence that encapsulates his mission and sums up the central theme and whole of Mark's Gospel: "The Son of Man did not come to be served but to serve and to give his life as a ransom for many" (Mk 10:45). It is Mark's equivalent to John's better known 3:16-17. Since ransom is paid for the redemption of captives and slaves, those imprisoned or in debt, the Good News, as Mark reports it, is that Jesus has come to redeem us all.

Today's Gospel also tells us something of the different styles and methods of the evangelists in their respective recording of the Gospel accounts. Mark wrote first. His is the shortest Gospel and in some ways the most primitive. There are few embellishments. Mark generally reported events as they unfolded and as the participants and bystanders understood the events at the time they took place. Mark shares little of the post-resurrection perspective and theologizing common to the later evangelists, especially John, and in this sense offers the most reliable firsthand or eye-witness accounts. In today' Gospel, for instance, Mark tells us James and John came directly to Jesus with their outrageous request. In Matthew's Gospel, by way of contrast, it is the mother of James and John who makes the request. Matthew apparently thought it too embarrassing for two of the Apostles to engage in such gross behavior and simply shifted blame to their hapless mother (Mt 20:20). Mark however was not afraid to tell things as they were. He, more than any other, dared describe things, warts and all.

Today's Gospel passage fittingly has a place in the liturgical cycle close to the Feast of All Saints. For today's Gospel provides the rationale for the feast. In today's Gospel we learn that the greatest in the kingdom of God are those who serve the needs of others on earth. In the Feast of All Saints we celebrate the countless men and women who served God faithfully and gloriously in their lifetimes by simply loving and caring for their families, friends, and fellow human beings. Though unknown and unsung by the world at large, nothing they did escaped God's notice and the universal Church celebrates the Feast of All Saints to acknowledge this fact and their individual greatness. Let us thank God for our deceased relatives and friends and for all they did for us. Let us ask God with confidence to reward them and welcome them into his glory.

Cure of Bartimaeus, the Blind Man

For the last two chapters of Mark Jesus has been making his way to Jerusalem where he will soon suffer and die. On the physical journey Jesus three times forewarns his Apostles of his upcoming passion and death in order to prepare them emotionally and spiritually for the ordeal he and they will have to face. But in each of his three attempts to open their eyes and minds to what is about to befall him in Jerusalem in fulfillment of God's plan, they fail dismally to see or comprehend what he is trying to tell them and prefer instead to stay lost in the dreamland of their own fantasies and illusions.

To highlight the Apostles' near willful and deliberate inability to see, Mark brackets the entire section between two rather remarkable cures of blind people. The first tells the unusual story of Jesus working patiently and in stages to help a blind man recover full use of his sight in the town of Bethsaida (Mk 8:22-26). Mark underscores Jesus' forbearance during the course of the miracle and his commitment to continue the curative process to its completion in order to foreshadow the equally extraordinary patience Jesus will demonstrate later towards the Apostles in three times repeating the imminence and inevitability of his passion, death, and resurrection. As the blind man of Bethsaida needed repeated help before he could see physically, so the Apostles would need sustained assistance before they could grasp or see what Jesus was trying to tell them of the critical role of suffering in his life and mission. The second story serving as the closing bracket is the one we read today.

The story of Bartimaeus is set in Jericho. Jericho was a city 23 miles east of Jerusalem. Some 3000 feet lower than Jerusalem and fed by an abundant spring called the Fountain of Elijah, it was a verdant garden spa where the wealthy went to wile away the winter. Situated near Israel's Jordan River border along the main trade route from the East, it was also the point of embarkation to the Holy Land for many a merchant and pilgrim. With Passover soon approaching, the road would be full of travelers heading for the Holy City. Wherever the rich gathered, wherever pilgrims trod, there were always beggars in search of alms. For there was no system of welfare or social assistance at the time. The handicapped and incapacitated subsisted solely on charity. Among the beggars one could expect many blind people. Blindness was deplorably widespread in the ancient Middle East. Its most common cause was a contagious infection of the cornea spread by ubiquitous flies and unsound hygienic habits.

Sitting by the roadside, Bartimaeus hears that Jesus is passing by and cries out, "Jesus, Son of David, have pity on me." He is the first person in Mark's Gospel to identify Jesus by the messianic title, Son of David. Despite opposition, he keeps calling out and forces Jesus' attention by persistence born of faith. Jesus asks him the very same question he asked of James and John in last week's Gospel, "What do you want me to do for you?" In marked contrast to Zebedee's sons who were naively unaware of their deep-rooted blindness concerning Jesus' true nature, Bartimaeus asks unequivocally to see. Mark uses the contrast to infer that had the Apostles been as aware of their spiritual blindness as Bartimaeus was of his physical blindness, Jesus might have been able to enlighten them of his mission sooner and more readily.

Because of Bartimaeus' great faith, the cure Jesus works takes place instantaneously on the level of both body and soul. As a sign of his deep faith and unwavering commitment, Bartimaeus' immediate response on regaining his sight is to follow Jesus up the road towards Jerusalem, a clear sign of true discipleship. Earlier he had thrown aside his cloak, a symbol of his old conduct and former way of life. The use of clothing to symbolize conduct is still found in the Church's baptismal rite today. The priest places a white garment on the child as a sign of its Christian dignity to be kept unsullied until eternal life.

It is noteworthy that Bartimaeus is the only person Jesus cured in the whole of Mark's Gospel who is identified by name. This may well suggest he remained a faithful follower of Jesus and was still known to the Christian community when Mark wrote his Gospel decades later. It is also notable that Jesus made no attempt to silence Bartimaeus when he addressed him publicly as Son of David. Unlike earlier incidents in which Jesus always promptly quelled any mention of him as Messiah, a practice later referred to as the Messianic Secret, Jesus now does nothing to stop this evident proclamation of his Messiahship. Some suggest that since he was approaching Jerusalem for the final time, the hour in which he would meet his passion and death, Jesus may have felt that the true nature of the Messiah as a suffering figure would soon be evident to all and consequently there was no longer any need to hide his true identity.

Restoration of sight in the Gospels was frequently used as a symbol for the awakening of faith. Many in the early Church saw in Bartimaeus' experience similarities with their own initial faith encounter. We can even find parallels today. (1) Bartimaeus was blind. He learns of Jesus only through hearsay. How important it is to have a Christian climate so people can hear of Jesus and be attracted by his ways. (2) Bartimaeus faces a hostile environment. When he called out to Jesus for help, Mark reports, "Many rebuked him, telling him to be silent" (Mk 10:48). The world frequently tries to distract us or discourage us from approaching God. (3) Bartimaeus resorts to courage. He shouts all the louder. If we are to draw closer to God, we have to work at it and be willing to buck the trend. (4) He receives encouragement from the followers of Jesus: "Take courage; get up, he is calling you" (Mk 10:49). We need others around us, family and friends, to help us draw closer to Jesus. (5) Bartimaeus throws aside his cloak to run the faster to Jesus. To live as Christians, we have to set many things aside, strip still other things away. (6) He receives a free invitation when Jesus asks him what he wants. It is a reminder that conversion is a free act, entered into only by choice. (7) His request is answered. Jesus gives him sight and faith. Our faith is also a free gift which helps us see more clearly and deeply. (8) Bartimaeus follows Jesus up the road to Jerusalem. We must also become his followers, willing to follow him even to Cavalry. (9) As one cured by Jesus, Bartimaeus gave witness in his person to God's goodness, mercy, and love. Through our lives and good deeds we are also called to give witness to God's love for us and for all the world.

The Greatest Commandment

Today's Gospel is based on the same incident reported in Matthew (22:34-40). Since this was treated in the Thirtieth Sunday of Year A, it leaves us free once again to explore the variations and differences among the evangelists in recalling and recording similar events.

Matthew's version of the encounter between Jesus and the scribe (lawyer) is sinister. The scribes and Pharisees had overcome their mutual dislike of the Sadducees and banded together with them to work against Jesus in a concerted attempt to bring him down. The Sadducees began the attack on Jesus with a question on the possibility of resurrection. They personally ridiculed the notion of an afterlife and refused to believe in it (cf. commentary for the Thirty-Second Sunday of the Year, Cycle C). Their question quickly backfired on them, however, due to Jesus' deft response (Mt 22:23-33). The scribes and Pharisees next took up the attack, represented by a scribe whom Matthew explicitly describes as hostile. The scribe asks Jesus about the greatest commandment for the expressed purpose of tripping him up. Luke (10:25-28) offers a similar setting, suggesting the scribe was definitely out to disconcert Jesus.

Mark alone among the Synoptic Gospels reports the scribe as sincere, open, and honestly inquisitive—one who was truly seeking enlightenment. Pious Jews were confronted with the 613 precepts of the Mosaic Law that were written down in the Torah and buttressed by thousands of man-made accretions recorded in the Talmud. Some, like the Pharisees, held that all the precepts were of equal importance and the whole law had to be observed in its entirety to achieve salvation. Others felt some hierarchy had to exist among the precepts, permitting distinctions between grave and light, or what we would term mortal and venial. Still others hoped to discover some overarching principle embedded in the law that would tie together the many precepts and render them easier to remember and put into practice.

Jesus did just that. In response to the man's honest inquiry, he goes straight to the heart of the law and sums it up in two principles: love of God and love of neighbor. The first commandment he picks comes from Deuteronomy (6:4-5): "Hear O Israel! The Lord is our God, the Lord alone. Therefore, you shall love the Lord, your God, with all your heart, and with all your soul, and with all your strength." Known as the *Shema* from the Hebrew word for *hear* which begins the passage, devout Jews recited it twice a day as a prayer, in the morning and in the evening, in the spirit of Deuteronomy (6:6-9). This same text also commanded them to inscribe the words in the little boxes, known as phylacteries, they wore on their arms and foreheads when they prayed and on the plaques, called mezuzahs, which they placed on the door posts and gates of their homes. This passage, then, was clearly central to Jewish thought and religion. Jesus simply showed it represented the kernel and full flowering of the whole Mosaic Law.

Since the Mosaic Law also abounded in obligations to other human beings, Jesus immediately enjoined a second command: "You shall love your neighbor as yourself." Once again Jesus stays within the Torah, part and parcel of divinely revealed Scripture. He selects Leviticus 19:18. The citation comes from a section in which Yahweh directs his people to be holy as Yahweh their God is holy. In example after example Yahweh makes clear the holiness he demands of them requires respect for their fellow human beings: the poor, the stranger, the underdog (Lv 19:1-37). Since there are also several specific references to "your own people," however, many rabbis opted for the path of least resistance and took "neighbor" to mean "fellow countrymen." In Luke's version of the story, Jesus therefore immediately follows this teaching with the Parable of the Good Samaritan in which he makes clear that neighbor includes everyone, even people like the Samaritans whom the Jews universally hated and despised as half-breeds and heretics.

As the initial environment for the exchange between Jesus and the scribe differed considerably between Mark and the other evangelists, so does the conclusion. In Matthew's account the scribe is silenced and dares not question Jesus further. In Luke's version the scribe presses ahead with a second question in an attempt to justify himself (10:29). In Mark's rendition, however, the scribe is deeply impressed with Jesus' response, even supportive of it. He praises Jesus and his insight in words that capture the essence of Hosea 6:6: "It is love I desire, not sacrifice," while at the same time echoing with amazing precision another teaching of Jesus. The scribe seconds Jesus' opinion and, uncharacteristic of the Pharisees who ranked outward observance above internal conversion, proclaims that love of God and love of neighbor are worth more than any ritual offering or sacrifice. Earlier Jesus had warned his disciples in the Sermon on the Mount, "If you bring your offering to the altar, and there recall that your brother has anything against you, leave your offering there at the altar, go first and be reconciled with your brother, and then come and offer your gift" (Mt 5: 23-24).

Evidently moved by the man's sincerity and similar, shared views, Jesus describes the scribe as not far from the kingdom of God. Mark's ending to the dialogue between Jesus and the scribe is reminiscent of the conclusion to the parable of the rich young man (Mk 10:17-30) which closed with Jesus looking on the young man with love. While the rich young man turned away sad because he had many possessions, we do not know what happened to the scribe. Perhaps he was able to follow his insights and break with the Pharisaic tradition; perhaps he was too deeply indoctrinated, too heavily entrenched.

The Widow's Mite

During the terrible conflict between the Hutus and Tutsis in Rwanda, a small band of refugees from one tribe stumbled into the path of a much larger group of refugees from the other tribe. Both groups were near the point of starvation but the children of the smaller group had found some edible roots which they gnawed on as they trudged along. The smaller group feared the larger group would attack them and take what little they had. But when the children of the larger group saw the children of the other group eating, they rushed forward and asked them for some of their food. It is an African custom to share and, though bitterly hungry themselves, the children of the badly outnumbered smaller group instinctively shared what little they had without question or complaint. The adults on both sides simply looked on from a distance and then moved on without altercation. The children's generosity had saved the day and in all likelihood the lives of their elders.

The first reading tells of a widow of Zarephath in the pagan territory of Phoenicia, a city which lay along the Mediterranean coast midway between Tyre and Sidon. The entire region was beset by famine, the result of a prolonged drought. In ancient times people were expected to offer hospitality to strangers, to open their homes and share their meals. This poor widow, with barely enough for her and her son to survive the day, willingly shared her last morsel of food with Elijah, a stranger and foreigner. Though a Gentile, she showed through her humanitarian gesture that deep reverence for God and love of neighbor existed even outside of Israel. For her extraordinary charity to a fellow human being in need, indicative of her complete trust in God, Elijah promises in God's name full sustenance for her and her son throughout the duration of the drought. As with the children in Rwanda, generosity to the point of seeming folly brings unexpected and extraordinary rewards.

The Gospel offers the moving account of the widow's mite. Widows in the ancient Jewish world had a difficult time. In this extended-family, male-dominated society, wives were not allowed to inherit their husband's estate. The husband's estate had to remain within the male line of the extended family. Daughters could inherit only if there were no sons, but they were then required to marry within the father's clan (Nb 36:8). In the absence of children, the estate would pass to the husband's brother, uncle, or nearest male kin. A widow without a grown son to inherit his father's estate and welcome her into *his* home, her *former* home, was in a sorry state. Frequently, like Naomi in the Book of Ruth, she would have to return to her own family, her own land, a ward to whoever would have her, with no source of income of her own. In today's Gospel the widow donates two small copper coins worth about a cent. It was all she had to live on.

Mark starts the account by telling us Jesus took a seat *opposite* the treasury. This provides both a graphic and attitudinal reference. For earlier Mark reported Jesus was so upset with the commerce in the Temple that he drove out the money changers and animal vendors (11:15). The Temple abounded with places to donate money. The sacred site consisted basically of three successive courtyards leading to the curtain cordoning off the Holy of Holies. The first upon entrance was the Court of the Gentiles, open to people of all faiths and of good will. The second was the Court of the Women, restricted to Jews, but of both sexes. The third was the Court of Men, accessible only to Jewish males. In the Court of Women alone there were thirteen trumpet-shaped containers, each carefully designated with the purpose of the donation: incense, doves, lambs, etc. The treasury building where the money was counted and stored was also located in the Court of the Women.

Earlier Jesus had castigated the Pharisees for their love of show. From other sources we know they frequently had someone blow a horn to call attention to any donation they were about to make. Their religious philosophy moreover pressured people to support the Temple and its services, even people like the widow who clearly couldn't afford it. The opulent running of the Temple meant more to them than any individual's personal need. Immediately after this passage, Jesus will speak of the Temple's destruction (13:1-2). Mark deliberately brackets the story of the widow's mite between these two passages of the Pharisees' love of show and the imminent demise of the Temple to highlight the nobility and pathos of the woman's gift. The Temple will pass, but the woman's sincerity and generosity will live on forever in God's sight and wherever the Gospel is preached. It is important to note, moreover, that Jesus does not use the story to urge us to give our last penny. He's clearly using the carrot, not the stick. The point of the story is simply to dramatize the fact that no act of charity ever passes unnoticed or goes unrewarded. As with the children of Rwanda and the widow of Zarephath, God will never be outdone in generosity.

As Christians we are called to imitate the generous love of the widow of Zarephath and the widow who gave her last mite. We are called to be generous with our time, talent, and treasure. Fortunately few of us are ever called to give of our sustenance, only of our surplus. But how generous are we even with our surplus? Before giving, most of us set aside enough for whatever we consider essential: the children's education, the summer/winter vacation, the night out on the town, the dog's veterinary bill—all important in themselves but things most people in the world can't even dream of. Much more than half the world has to struggle each day, often unsuccessfully, simply to feed their children and put a roof over their heads. God doesn't ask for our last penny, but can we and should we do more than we are doing?

And how about our country? We often think of ourselves as the most generous country on earth and in many ways we are. We give the most in absolute terms but relative to our GDP we give barely 1%, while most developed countries give 2% of their GDPs. And much of our aid is tied to military assistance. Catholic Relief Services published three interesting statistics for the year 2000. (1)

It would take $13 billion a year to feed all of the world's hungry. To put this figure in perspective, the U.S. and Europe together spend $17 billion a year on pet food. (2) It would cost $6 billion a year to educate all of the world's children with no access to schooling and hence little hope to escape poverty. The U.S. spends $8 billion a year simply on cosmetics. (3) The three wealthiest men in the world have more money that all the people in the 48 poorest countries in the world combined. The *New York Times* reported independently that it would cost $6 billion a year to provide the world with safe drinking water and thus prevent hundreds of thousands of deaths each year, mostly of children, from dysentery. A huge sum, but less than half of what we spend each year on alcoholic beverages alone.

Today's readings challenge us as individuals and as a nation. While we need not bleed ourselves or our country dry, we ought at least scrutinize our personal and national priorities.

Apocalyptic Happenings

Each year as the fall season comes to an end, the liturgical year also draws to a close. Next Sunday will be the feast of Christ the King, the last Sunday of this liturgical year. The Sunday after that will be the First Sunday of Advent, the start of a new liturgical year. And every year at this time, no matter what the cycle, the Church asks us to consider the last things, the end of time. Scientists agree the world as we know it will one day pass away. It may be billions of years away according to their calculations, but it will pass away. The Church simply asks us to reflect on that inevitability, even though no one expects it soon, so that we may always be ready to greet God when he summons us. For while the end of the world is in all likelihood not imminent, we have no such surety over the timing of our own death. The Church's point in offering this eschatological theme of the end of the world is never to scare us, only to prepare us.

Our first reading is from the Book of Daniel. The Book of Daniel is classified with the prophetic literature in the Old Testament but it is really closer in style to apocalyptic literature. Apocalypse means unveiling, a drawing aside of the curtain that hides the future from sight. Generally written during times of persecution, apocalyptic literature seeks to interpret the present in terms of the future, to provide solace and insight amid current difficulties by offering hope for and assurances of better things and times to come. Since it was written during times of persecution, the language is often obscure, deliberately veiled. To protect the author and anyone caught reading the book, symbols were used to conceal the true identity of individuals and nations; mystical numbers employed to obfuscate dates. Only those privy to the coded data could interpret its true meaning, making it deliberately difficult for the enemy. Unfortunately, however, it also poses problems for us today who come much later to the literature and are no longer familiar with the codes and symbols.

The Book of Daniel was written during the reign of Antiochus IV, who ruled over the Holy Land from 175-164 BC. In an effort to unite his far-flung empire, he tried to impose a universal religion and culture on the many peoples and diverse regions over which he ruled. A major problem, however, was that he considered himself a principal god in his new syncretic religion and insisted Greek ways or Hellenism be the dominant culture. This led to persistent problems and persecutions for the Jews who clung tenaciously to their monotheistic faith in Yahweh and their practice of Jewish customs and traditions. Enraged by their stalwart resistance, Antiochus retaliated by plundering the Temple of its sacred objects, erecting a statue of Zeus in the heart of the Temple precinct, and decreeing that all Jews had to worship this pagan idol under pain of death. Details of the unspeakable suffering that ensued are recorded in the First and Second Books of Maccabees.

Our first reading comes from the last of Daniel's four visions. The time of "unsurpassed distress" refers to the persecution by Antiochus IV. To rouse flagging Jewish spirits, Daniel makes mention of Michael, the archangel revered as the special protector of the Jewish people. With his heavenly help, Daniel intimates, the powers of this mad diabolical pagan prince cannot long endure. There is hope in the offing for those currently suffering. And for those who have already fallen victim to this terrible persecution, "those who sleep in the dust of the earth," there is also hope. In one of the earliest and strongest references to the resurrection of the body in the Old Testament, Daniel stoutly avers that those who have perished in the persecution will awake and shine brightly, that they will live forever and be like stars in the firmament (Dn 12:2-3).

Today's Gospel is part of what is commonly called the Eschatological Discourse, but its tone is decidedly more apocalyptic in nature. While most commentators believe Jesus is speaking of the end of the world, some think he is referring to the destruction of the Temple; others, the persecutions that would follow. The apocalyptic imagery would seem to best fit this last interpretation, as does Jesus' conclusion. According to this view, the imagery of the sun being darkened, the moon not giving light, and the stars falling from the sky, is not meant to be taken literally and so does not refer to the world's end. The imagery is rather an attempt to capture the earth-shaking effects of persecution, things so horrible that people's worlds would indeed seem to be unraveling and coming to an end. Here Jesus forewarns his disciples of persecutions, not to frighten them but to fortify them with the assurance that they too will one day pass.

Using the title, Son of Man from the Book of Daniel (7:13-14), Jesus promises to come upon the clouds and gather his chosen ones from the four winds. He tells them that when these things happen the end is near. In apocalyptic literature the end typically refers to the end of the persecution, not the end of the world. Hence what Jesus is saying according to this interpretation is that persecutions will invariably come but Jesus will return to be with his Church and the persecutions will eventually end. Jesus further asserts the present generation will not pass away until all this happens. Mark's community did indeed know persecution, from both the Jewish religious authorities and the Roman Empire. Both eventually ceased, however, and by 314 AD Christianity had become the official religion of the Roman Empire. Jesus also fulfilled his promise to return within the lifetime of his contemporaries, moreover, not in the Second Coming as many erroneously expected, but in the resurrection. Scripture attests that when raised from the dead, Jesus returned and appeared to his disciples and the early Church in glory. Our faith tells us he continues to remain with the Church even to this day through his abiding presence in the sacraments and Eucharist and that he will come again one day to judge the living and the dead.

The Son Of Man

Today is the feast of Christ the King. While Jesus often spoke of the Kingdom of God, it is interesting and informative that he never used the image of king for himself in his preaching. Judging from usage, the image he felt best described his role in God's plan of salvation was the Son of Man. We find the origin of that image in today's first reading from the Book of Daniel. Since Son of Man is the only Old Testament title that Jesus appropriated to himself and it is unquestionably the one he used most frequently for himself, it would seem worthwhile to examine how the title originated, what precisely it means, and what connotations and colorations it developed over the course of the centuries. The endeavor will also afford us an opportunity to peer into the Book of Daniel, which is rarely assigned for a Sunday reading.

The Book of Daniel was written sometime between 168 and 163 BC during the persecution of the Jews by Antiochus IV. Though listed under the prophets, the Book of Daniel is better described as part of the apocalyptic literature. Apocalyptic literature prevailed during times of persecution, political unrest, and social upheaval. It was typically written to strengthen the faith of people suffering for their religion and to encourage them to persevere. For the safety of both author and reader the message was enciphered in codes and symbols to render it unintelligible to the enemy. What worked so well against the enemy then, however, now frustrates many modern readers who are no longer privy to the symbols.

The Jewish people had a long history of oppression and persecution. Assyria conquered the ten northern tribes of Israel in 722 BC and consigned them to a disastrous exile that obliterated their national, racial, and religious entity. They simply disappeared from history and are known as the ten lost tribes of Israel. Babylon conquered the two remaining southern tribes in 587 BC and similarly sent them off into exile. In 539 BC the Persians and Medes under Cyrus the Great defeated Babylon in a decisive battle that allowed the Jewish exiles to return home and establish a vassal state. In 336 BC the Greeks under Alexander the Great routed the Persians and took over their empire. When he died shortly thereafter, his generals quickly divvied up his empire. Of the Middle East portion, Ptolemy grabbed Egypt where he founded a long-lasting dynasty and Seleucus commandeered the regions of Syria and Mesopotamia where his progeny would cling to power for generations.

At the time the Book of Daniel was written Palestine was ruled by a scion of the Seleucid dynasty. Of the endless line of conquerors and subjugators Israel was forced to endure, Antiochus IV proved the worst. He sought to unify his empire by imposing a common religion and culture with himself as a prominent deity and Greek mores as the dominant lifestyle. Both violated Jewish law and custom, setting occupier and occupied on a collision course. Irked by Jewish resistance to his master plan, Antiochus made a capital crime of such things as reading or owning the Torah, having a son circumcised, refusing to adore the statue of the Greek god Zeus that he had provocatively installed before the very Holy of Holies. As a result, the Jewish people were suffering as never before.

Today's first reading which speaks of the Son of Man starts with a vision in which Daniel recounts Israel's long history of oppression using symbols for safety (7:1-7). Since the ten northern tribes were already lost to history, he focuses on the two southern tribes of Judah and begins with the Babylonian conquest. In his vision he sees four beasts emerge from the sea, which in ancient times was considered the dwelling place of Satan, his evil spirits, and most malevolent forces. The beasts are all ferocious. The first was like a lion with eagle's wings, suggesting Babylon which used a similar figure as a royal insignia and painted the emblem on its city gates and palace walls. The second beast was like a bear gnawing on three ribs protruding from its mouth. A ruthless, powerful predator, the bear served as a symbol for the Medes.

The third beast was like a leopard with bird's wings and four heads. The leopard symbolized Persia; the wings, the speed with which it rose to power; the four heads, its four leaders before its sudden and unexpected collapse: Cyrus, Xerxes, Artaxerxes, and Darius. The fourth and last beast, the most terrifying of all, sported iron teeth, ten horns, and a small, newer horn sprouting from its brow. This last, nearly indescribable figure portrays the Greeks, of whom Antiochus IV was the current ruler. The ten horns represent the ten previous Seleucid rulers; the new horn, Antiochus IV. The iron teeth signify that the beast is designed and equipped by nature to devour everything in its path.

Amid this terror the Ancient One appears with the court of heaven. In biblical time old age was revered. Applied to a monarch it suggested staying power and hence legitimacy. In the case of God it evoked the eternal nature of God's kingdom in contrast to the transitory character of human rule. The books of heaven are opened in which humankind's actions are recorded. Judgment follows immediately. The fourth and worst beast is killed and the other three stripped of their power. With these evil influences eliminated, Daniel then sees one like a son of man coming on the clouds. To him God gives glory, kingship, and dominion over all people. The image originally applied to Israel which would rule, not like a beast as previous nations, but as a human being, a son of man. Jewish opinion, however, soon turned the son of man image into a glorious messiah figure, one who would liberate them and exercise dominance over the Gentiles. In claiming the title as his own, Jesus reverts to the original intent. His rule will be humane, not beastly. His every use of the image, while always expressing power, connotes kindness, gentleness, service. He has come "not to be served, but to serve" (Mk 10:45). Without murmur or complaint, like the Suffering Servant of Isaiah, he will freely lay down his life for us that we might enjoy eternal life forever with his Father.